W9-AAV-785

necklaceology

candie cooper

necklaceology

How to Make Chokers, Lariats, Ropes & More

LARK CRAFTS

Asheville

EDITOR
Nathalie Mornu

COPY EDITOR
Karen Levy

ART DIRECTOR
Kathleen Holmes

BOOK & COVER DESIGN
Pamela Norman

PROJECT PHOTOGRAPHY
Stewart O'Shields

HOW-TO PHOTOGRAPHY
Candie Cooper

ILLUSTRATORS
Candie Cooper
Bernadette Wolf

EDITORIAL ASSISTANCE
Hannah Doyle

EDITORIAL INTERNS
Alex Alesi
Virginia Roper

LARK CRAFTS

An Imprint of Sterling Publishing
387 Park Avenue South
New York, NY 10016

If you have questions or comments about this book, please visit: larkcrafts.com

Library of Congress Cataloging-in-Publication Data

Cooper, Candie, 1979-

Necklaceology : how to make chokers, lariats, ropes & more / Candie Cooper. -- First Edition.

    pages cm

Includes index.

ISBN 978-1-4547-0333-4

1. Beadwork. 2. Necklaces.
3. Jewelry making. I. Title.

  TT860.C6627 2012

  745.5942--dc23

    2012000145

10 9 8 7 6 5 4 3 2 1

First Edition

Published by Lark Crafts
An Imprint of Sterling Publishing Co., Inc.
387 Park Avenue South, New York, NY 10016

Text © 2012, Candie Cooper
Project photography © 2012, Lark Crafts, an Imprint of Sterling Publishing Co., Inc.
How-to photography © 2012, Candie Cooper
Illustrations © 2012, Candie Cooper

Distributed in Canada by Sterling Publishing, c/o Canadian Manda Group, 165 Dufferin Street Toronto, Ontario, Canada M6K 3H6

Distributed in the United Kingdom by GMC Distribution Services, Castle Place, 166 High Street, Lewes, East Sussex, England BN7 1XU

Distributed in Australia by Capricorn Link (Australia) Pty Ltd.,P.O. Box 704, Windsor, NSW 2756 Australia

The written instructions, photographs, designs, patterns, and projects in this volume are intended for the personal use of the reader and may be reproduced for that purpose only. Any other use, especially commercial use, is forbidden under law without written permission of the copyright holder.

Every effort has been made to ensure that all the information in this book is accurate. However, due to differing conditions, tools, and individual skills, the publisher cannot be responsible for any injuries, losses, and other damages that may result from the use of the information in this book.

Manufactured in China

All rights reserved

ISBN 13: 978-1-4547-0333-4

For information about custom editions, special sales, and premium and corporate purchases, please contact the Sterling Special Sales Department at specialsales@sterlingpub.com or 800-805-5489.

Requests for information about desk and examination copies available to college and university professors must be submitted to academic@larkbooks.com. Our complete policy can be found at www.larkcrafts.com.

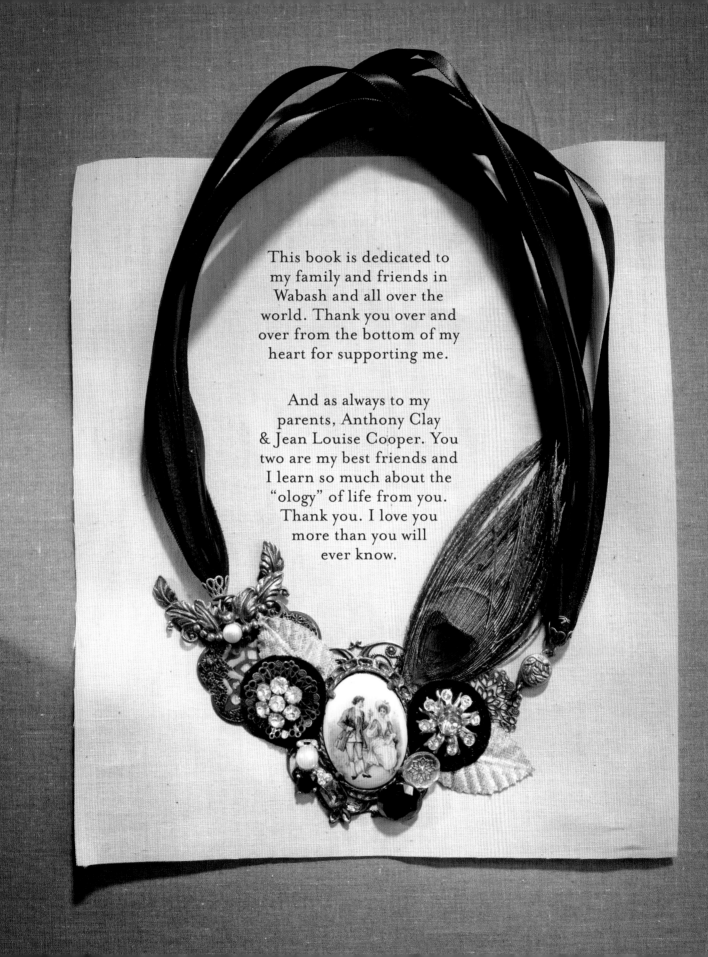

This book is dedicated to my family and friends in Wabash and all over the world. Thank you over and over from the bottom of my heart for supporting me.

And as always to my parents, Anthony Clay & Jean Louise Cooper. You two are my best friends and I learn so much about the "ology" of life from you. Thank you. I love you more than you will ever know.

contents

collars & chokers

princess-length baubles

marvelous matinées

elegant operas

ropes to twirl & spin

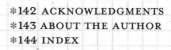

materials & tools

JEWELRY IS MEANT to accentuate your figure and your attire. Not every shirt looks good on the same person, right? Well, not all necklaces look good on the same body type. It's little things like this that make the world go 'round, giving us our individual style.

Consider this book of 40 projects a playful study of necklace making. It's a light-hearted field guide that teaches everything about creating chokers, princess-length necklaces, ropes, and more. You'll find boxes called "Experiment" that suggest ways you can alter the designs. Others called "Analyze the Data" point out special features. Each style of necklace has correlating measurements; I've therefore organized the projects into chapters based on their dimensions. Certain lengths look better with different necklines. I always have to look in the mirror, trying necklaces on until I see which one "works"!

collar

Collar-length necklaces are 12 to 13 inches (30.5 to 33 cm) long and fit snugly around the neck. Barbara Streisand wears them so beautifully! Or do you remember the Parisian look with the little black ribbon and cameo? Collars are flat, so they stay up against your neck easily.

choker

Choker-length necklaces are 14 to 16 inches (35.6 to 40.6 cm) long. This length makes me think of a classic strand of knotted pearls.

princess

Add a couple of inches and you get the extremely popular princess-length necklace. I believe the Hope Diamond, which went through many transformations before it ended up at the Smithsonian, is a princess-length necklace.

Princess necklaces are 17 to 19 inches (43.2 to 48.3 cm) long, making them hang just below the throat.

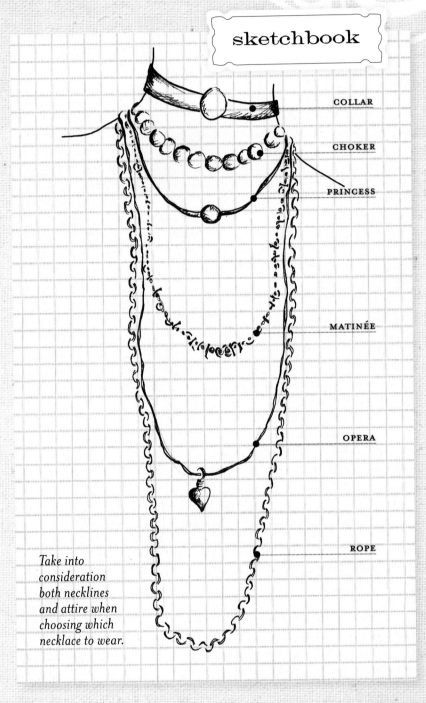

sketchbook

COLLAR

CHOKER

PRINCESS

MATINÉE

OPERA

ROPE

Take into consideration both necklines and attire when choosing which necklace to wear.

matinée

If you have a necklace 20 to 24 inches (50.8 to 61 cm) long, then you have a matinée-length necklace. If you wear this style, go with plain casual or business dress and let the necklace be the decoration for your outfit.

opera

The elegant opera-length necklace is 28 to 34 inches (71.1 to 86.4 cm) long. I love this length because you can wear it doubled or as a single strand. Leis and Mardi Gras beads are opera-length necklaces.

rope

A rope-length necklace is 45 inches (1.1 m) long. You can double and sometimes triple this length! Remember the flappers swinging a knotted strand of pearls around? That is a rope-length necklace. This necklace accentuates the torso.

So what will you need to make necklaces yourself?

beads

There are so many options for beads and findings. You know this if you've dabbled at all in jewelry making. At the end of the day, my advice is this: if you like it and it makes you happy, make a piece of jewelry with it!

Beads come in a ton of different shapes and I buy beads everywhere I go. I mean everywhere! It will be a miracle if I use half of them before I leave the planet. I find them at craft stores, online, at bead and trade shows, during my travels, in old necklaces from yard sales ... the list

goes on. I have a couple of questions I ask myself when buying beads for projects. What's the project? If it's a bridal piece, it may be handed down to another generation, so I go with beautiful, high-quality components, such as pearls and crystals. If the piece is trendy—here today, gone tomorrow—I can get by with less expensive components (in my humble opinion). Here are a few extra details about some of the beads used in this book.

seed & bugle beads ❶

Seed beads are simply very tiny beads. They come in sizes indicated by 1/0, 4/0, 6/0, and so on. (Instead, you might see beads labeled 1°, 4°, 6°, and so forth. Both symbols mean the same thing, and both are pronounced "ott.") The smaller the number, the bigger the bead. Bugle beads are also very tiny, except they come in a tube shape. You can purchase these beads loosely or in hanks, which are bundles of strands.

gemstones ❷

I think gemstones add a whole new level of sophistication to designs. They come in different cuts and color qualities, which determine the price. You may notice there are grades next to the name, such as AA grade or B grade. As you probably guessed, AA grade is better than B grade. At the end of the day, you need to examine what you're buying and make sure you're getting a fair

price. I like to hit the bead shows and buy $5 strands of the tiny chips. If you want to add symbolism to your designs, gemstones are a good choice because they have many meanings that you can uncover with a little research.

decorative metal beads ❸

Metal beads come in all shapes and sizes. Using them in designs will add a nice amount of weight to the piece. Metal looks good next to anything, so

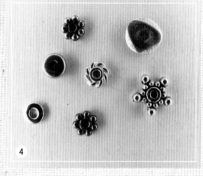

HELIX

ROUND

RONDELLE

BICONE

BRIOLETTE

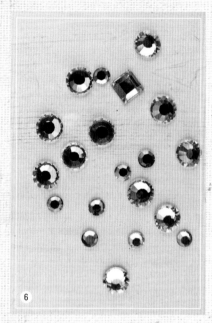

flat–back crystals ❻

Flat-back crystals are just what they sound like—one side is flat so that they can be glued to bezel settings or other beads for further embellishment.

wooden beads ❼

Wooden beads can come stained, the way furniture is, or unfinished. Buy unfinished if you want to paint and decorate them yourself. You can also buy stained beads and sand the finish to remove it or make it look rustic. You might even find some printed wooden beads.

czech glass beads ❽

I used Czech beads in some of my first beaded creations. They're made in the Czech Republic, land of beautiful glass beads in all shapes and sizes. They come in fire-polished, cathedral cuts, and drakes, to name a few. My favorite Czech glass technique is found

you can't go wrong purchasing a pack or two.

metal spacer beads ❹

One of my philosophies in jewelry making is "no spacer bead left behind." I use them to create a layered feel and to tie everything together. If you're going to purchase just one or two packs, I suggest opting for plain brass and silver.

crystals ❺

What makes true crystal beads so beautiful is their clarity and precise, machine-cut facets. Crystals come in a rainbow of colors as well as sizes. Bicone, round, helix, twists, briolettes, and rondelles are just some of the cuts you'll find. Some crystals have a coating on them, too. For example, if you see AB next to the crystal name, it has an iridescent Aurora Borealis coating. Heed my warning: Using one crystal will lead to using tons because the contrast with other beads adds so much interest!

FIRE-POLISHED

PRESSED GLASS

DRAKE

CATHEDRAL CUT

8

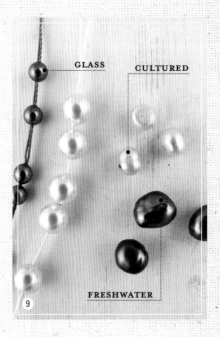

GLASS   CULTURED

FRESHWATER

9

in pressed-glass beads. These beads have been molded into shapes such as bugs, leaves, butterflies, and abstract designs. The colors of Czech glass beads are amazing.

cultured pearls, freshwater pearls & glass pearls ❾

Pearls can be man-made and/or nature-made. Truly natural pearls are rare and very costly. Most pearls are farmed, from pearl oysters (these are called cultured pearls) and freshwater mussels (freshwater pearls). Freshwater pearls tend to have a more irregular form than the round cultured pearls, and they come in a wide variety of shapes, colors, and sizes. Glass pearls are nice because the colors are radiant and the shape is perfectly round (you can find them in other shapes as well). I love pearls for their organic, satin look.

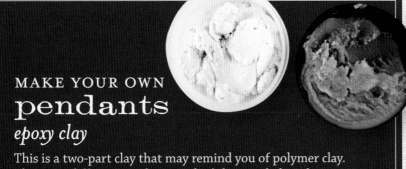

MAKE YOUR OWN
pendants
epoxy clay

This is a two-part clay that may remind you of polymer clay. The main difference is that you don't have to bake it because it self-hardens. You'll need a bezel frame finding to contain the clay and embellishments. There are different working times for each brand of clay, and they come in many colors. I like using white because you can stain it with acrylic paint to highlight texture and such. You can also stain any of the premade colors with paint or alcohol inks.

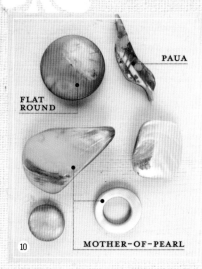

FLAT
ROUND

PAUA

MOTHER-OF-PEARL

10

CERAMIC

RESIN

CLOISONNÉ

11

shell beads 10

Other beads with an organic feel are made from paua (abalone from New Zealand), mother-of-pearl, and lip shell. Shell beads come in a variety of cuts as well as laminated fragments of shell on a base bead. Depending on the shell, the finish can be matte or iridescent.

cloisonné, ceramic & resin beads 11

Native to Asia, cloisonné beads are available in various qualities. Cloisonné is made by fusing tiny wires to a base and then pouring glass enamel into the separate compartments. The colors of these beads tend to be bright and beautiful. Ceramic beads are good for an earthy appeal. I also like them because they often have large holes, which are perfect for hemp or other thick cording. Resin beads are some-times referred to as Lucite. These beautiful acrylic beads look great in the light because of their transparency.

12

13

felt beads 12

Felt beads are a fun, lightweight alternative to glass beads. You can buy them with or without holes. It's easy to put holes in felt beads with an awl. Use them as is or embellish with stitching and seed beads.

filigree pieces 13

Filigree is good alone or in clusters. You can rivet pieces to it, hammer it, paint it, and so on. My favorite thing is to hammer it and then rivet lots of layers together with a mini nut and bolt.

findings

Findings, such as clasps, head pins, eye pins, jump rings, wire guards, crimp

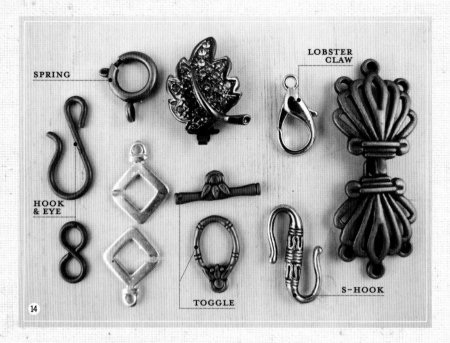

SPRING

LOBSTER CLAW

HOOK & EYE

TOGGLE

S-HOOK

14

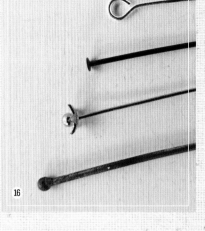

16

15

17

beads, and more, are the mechanisms that make strands of beads into wearable jewelry. They come in a variety of metals, including base metal, silver plated, sterling silver, gold, brass, and pewter, as well as finishes, such as gunmetal, brushed, and antiqued, to name a few. Choosing findings is much like choosing beads. It all depends on the quality of the project and the look you wish to achieve.

clasps ⓮ ⓯

The clasp is the mechanism that closes the necklace. If the necklace is long enough, it doesn't need a clasp. When closed, some clasps, such as toggle clasps, retain their distinctive two parts, while others, such as box clasps, look like they're one piece. Some of the clasps you'll find in this book are hook and eye, S hook, hook, spring, lobster claw, toggle, and box.

head pins & eye pins ⓰

Head pins are little wires onto which you string beads to create dangles and charms. You can buy them premade or you can make your own balled head pins using copper, fine silver, or sterling silver wire and a torch. Eye pins are wires with a simple loop on the end. You also buy them or make them yourself with wire and round-nose pliers.

jump rings ⓱

I've heard so many folks call jump rings "jumpers." I like it. Jump rings are metal rings with openings in them to connect clasps, charms, chains, and the like. They come in different shapes and finishes depending on the look you want. I like square and round jump rings best.

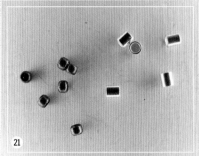

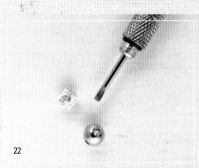

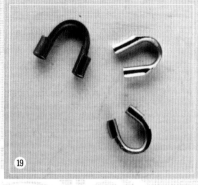

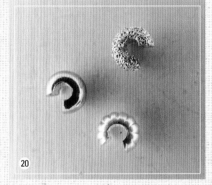

solid rings ⓲

You'll find solid rings used many times in the projects. They come in a variety of shapes and metals. The benefit to using solid rings is that there's no opening, so they're very secure. This makes them especially good for charms or the loop end of a clasp; jump rings are better suited for making connections, such as attaching clasps.

wire guards ⓳

Wire guards are U-shaped findings with a track that your beading wire can run along. A fitting name, the wire guard protects the wire from high-stress areas, so it won't get worn through.

crimp bead covers ⓴, crimp beads ㉑ & scrimp findings ㉒

Some of the beadwork in this book will be finished with crimp beads or crimp tubes and others with the perhaps less familiar crimp findings called Scrimps.

Crimp beads come in bead or tube shapes and a variety of sizes. The size you need depends on the diameter of your wire. The packaging on your wire will tell you what size crimp bead you need. Scrimps are small beads with screws that loosen and tighten to secure the wire inside them. A miniature screwdriver will come with your Scrimps so you can easily secure the screw inside. I sometimes choose Scrimps over crimp beads because they don't accidentally crack like crimp beads sometimes do and I can easily

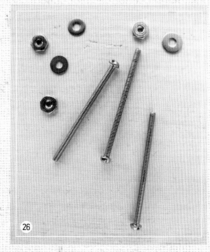

adjust the length before cutting the wire. I also like them because, depending on the design, they blend in better. Of course, you can always use a crimp bead cover to hide the end connection and make it more decorative.

clamshells ㉓, fold–over end findings ㉔ & bead tips ㉕

Clamshells, bead tips, and fold-over end findings are for finishing the ends of cords and ribbons so you can attach a clasp or other finding securely. The type of cord or ribbon you're using will determine which end finding to use. Clamshells and bead tips are good for delicate silk and nylon cord as well as WireLace. Fold-over ends are good for thick cord, ribbon, and suede lace. For glue-in findings, you'll want to use a precision-tip applicator to avoid getting glue on your stringing material.

miniature nuts & bolts ㉖

These are essentially miniature screws. I use them to stack and connect pieces to create pendants and charms. You can pick them up from hobby supply shops or online.

chain ㉗

I love chain! Chain comes in all different sizes and finishes—brass, copper, silver-plated, even polyester-covered. You can

also buy decorative commercial beaded chain. Sometimes the links are soldered shut and sometimes they're open. It seems I never leave the craft store without a package (or two) of chain.

cup chain ㉘

Cup chain is flexible chain that has rhinestones or crystals set into tiny bezels along the chain. You can purchase the chain in various sizes, metal colors, and color combinations. For the

29

31

30

32

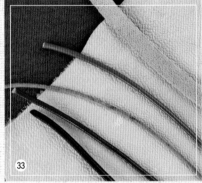

33

projects in this book, you'll also need to purchase the special cup chain end findings with loops so you can connect the chain to jump rings.

wire

Wire comes in a variety of metals, shapes, hardnesses, and sizes. Again, what you're making determines what you should purchase. There's copper, brass, sterling silver, and color-coated craft wire. Wire also comes in different shapes, such as round, square, and flat, as well as a number of hardnesses. Dead-soft wire indicates the wire can be easily bent; half-hard wire is more rigid. Memory wire is tempered steel, so it holds its shape. It comes in coils for rings, necklaces, and bracelets. The diameter of wire is indicated in gauges. In all cases, the smaller the gauge number, the thicker the wire. If you plan to make your own head pins, use the wire specified in the project instructions.

stringing materials

Beads can be strung onto a number of different materials, including beading wire, ribbon, silk cording, yarn, hemp, nylon, WireLace, and leather. The material you select will determine the overall look and style of the piece.

beading wire 29

Beading wire is what you string beads onto, and it isn't at all the same as regular wire. If you were to take a cross-section of beading wire you'd see that it actually consists of a bunch of tiny strands of wire twisted together to make one wire. The number of strands used and the diameter of the finished wire are indicated on the package. The more strands twisted into the single wire, the more flexible the wire. For example, 49-strand

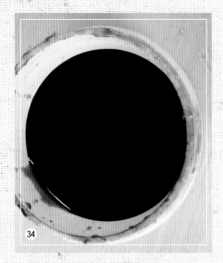

34

35

wire is more flexible than 19-strand wire. The diameter comes in .010, .012, .013, .015, .018, .021, and .024 inch (.250, .305, .330, .381, .457, .525, and .610 mm). Check the holes in your beads before selecting the wire's diameter. You'll also see the beading wire package indicates the weight at which the wire will break. Again, look at your beads to determine what works for your project. This is especially important when working with chunky gemstones or glass beads. Selecting the right beading wire for your project is important because it's essentially the foundation for your piece. My favorite all-purpose wire is 49-strand .018-inch (.46 mm) wire. Another thing you'll find is that beading wire comes in a range of colors. You may incorporate those wire colors in your design. I like selecting wire that blends in, as seen in Plum Tree (page 78).

ribbon & silk cording ㉚

In the projects in this book, you'll find hand-dyed silk ribbon, vintage lace, recycled silk ribbon, and various other ribbons incorporated into the designs. I especially like how the texture of ribbon contrasts with the cold, slick

beads. Silk cording can be purchased from bead supply stores online. It's very delicate and tubular and comes in a wide range of colors.

yarn, hemp & nylon ㉛

Whereas ribbon and silk cording provide more of a decorative element in my designs, I use crocheted yarn, knotted hemp, and nylon as foundational materials. There are some really beautiful novelty yarns that are simply perfect on their own. Hemp comes in many colors; you'll see a contemporary spin on macramé in Peace Dreams (page 139). Nylon is great for knotting and crocheting.

wirelace ㉜

WireLace is made of delicate woven wires that create a lacy-looking strand or tube. You can fill the tube with beads, or crochet with the fine strands. WireLace comes in different widths and the most delicious colors; it can be purchased from online jewelry-making suppliers.

leather ㉝

To create a rustic look for your necklace, try working some leather into your design. It comes in flat and round cording as well as sheets in a variety of colors. Flat ribbonlike leather is sometimes called suede lace. You can cut leather easily with scissors or on a self-healing mat with a craft knife. Available at your local craft store, leather can be painted or dyed if you can't find a specific color.

finishes

Knowing how to apply finishes to metal can add a customized feel to your pieces even if you're using commercial findings. It also helps make all the findings blend together, creating a cohesive look.

liver of sulfur ㉞

I love finishing metal findings with liver of sulfur, an easy-to-use chemical that oxidizes, or antiques, copper, brass, and silver surfaces. I started out using it in rock form and now I've switched to gel. As you work through the projects, you'll notice that I toss many of my jewelry components into a liver of sulfur bath to knock off the high shine. After polishing, the recessed areas remain darker, thus highlighting the detail work.

enamel paints ㉟

You can purchase enamel paints in spray and brush-on form. It all depends on the look you want. Spray paints are great for an even coat of pigment. Brush-on paints are good for adding dots and rubbing on a piece to highlight texture.

36

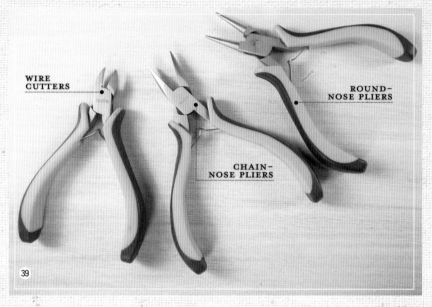

WIRE CUTTERS

ROUND-NOSE PLIERS

CHAIN-NOSE PLIERS

39

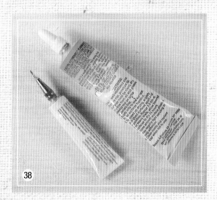

37

38

abrasives & polishing compounds ③⑦

There are two abrasives I use over and over. One is 220-grit sandpaper and the other is pumice powder. You can buy sandpaper from any hardware store in a variety of coarsenesses. The higher the number, the finer the grit. In other words, 1500-grit sandpaper is extremely smooth compared to 220-grit sandpaper. Pumice powder is a 320-grit fine powder that can be used to clean and remove oxidation from metal surfaces. I use it in conjunction with liver of sulfur. It's nontoxic and biodegradable.

adhesives ③⑧

There are so many adhesives on the market for jewelry makers. Ask any pro which is his or her favorite, and you'll get a different answer every time. Take the project into consideration when selecting an adhesive and check the packaging to see whether it's suitable. I like epoxy glues that come with precision tips. This makes gluing beads along a strand much easier. If it doesn't have a precision tip, you can always apply it with a toothpick. I will say to stay away from super glue—it clouds glass and becomes brittle.

tools

Curves, twirls, and depth can be added to your metal pieces by using forming tools. Some basic tools you'll need for all the projects are jeweler's wire cutters, chain-nose pliers, round-nose pliers, and crimping pliers. There's a vast assortment of jeweler's pliers, and I've found that if you plan on doing a lot of jewelry making, it's best to get a set of ergonomic-grip pliers. Whether this is a hobby or part of your income, it's good to take care of your joints and muscles! Other tools, such as a butane torch or a pearl knotter, are useful for certain projects.

wire cutters ③⑨

I like to have a good pair and a grubby pair of wire cutters on my workbench.

alcohol inks ③⑥

Alcohol inks have changed my jewelry-making life! With all the different metal colors and brightnesses of these inks, you can make anything blend. They come in a wide range of colors and go on transparent, so they tint the metal in whatever color you like. The brown tones are my favorite.

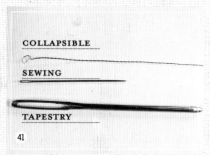

40

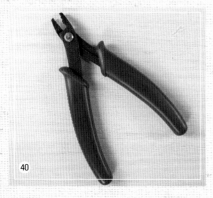

COLLAPSIBLE

SEWING

TAPESTRY

41

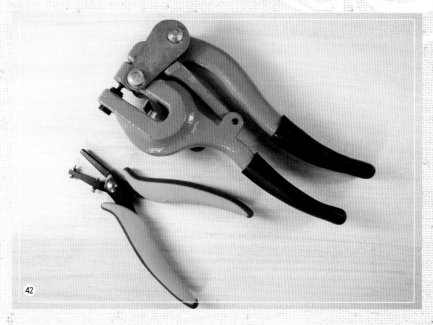

42

I use the good pair for snipping copper and silver wire. The grubby pair is used for snipping apart vintage jewelry components or heavy-gauge wire. Never use your good set for snipping memory wire because memory wire is tempered steel and will put nicks in your cutters!

chain-nose pliers ③⑨

Chain-nose pliers have a tapered nose, which makes them good for getting into tight spaces. If you can swing it, two pairs of these come in handy for opening and closing loops and jump rings.

round-nose pliers ③⑨

The nose on round-nose pliers is—you guessed it—round! Use this pair for forming loops and twirls.

crimping pliers ④⓪

Crimping pliers are for securing crimp beads to wires. They have two openings in the jaw of the pliers, one for flattening the crimp bead and one for rolling it shut.

needles ④①

A few different needles are used in this book. Some are for stitching and some for stringing.

● A **collapsible beading needle** makes stringing beads onto nylon really easy because the eye closes (hence its name) so it can slide through beads with small holes.

● A **sewing needle** is used to embellish surfaces with thread and seed beads.

● A **tapestry needle** is heavier and has a large eye, so you can thread multiple strands of cord or ribbon, as well as elastic cord and similar materials, and go through large-holed beads.

hole-punching tools ④②

I'm so excited about the really clever tools on the market today for punching holes in metal. It's so easy now with metal hand punches. **Punches** come in many sizes and shapes, and I like them because they make a clean hole, unlike drilling with a drill bit. You can pick them up at specialty jewelry supply companies, craft stores, and some hardware stores. A **handheld electric drill** with a chuck is useful for drilling thick and alternative materials, such as wood or steel keys. Tiny drill bits can be purchased at a hardware store or jewelry supply company. Make sure the drill bits you purchase are for metal (rather than wood) to make drilling easy. In this book I used 1/16-inch (1.5 mm) bits.

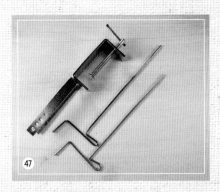

bead stoppers

There is no worse sound than when a strand of beads slides off the end of a wire and hits the floor. Bead stoppers can prevent this by temporarily securing beads on a wire. These nifty gadgets look like little springs with handles. Look for them anywhere beads are sold.

bead boards & bead mats

Bead boards have measurements and ridges in place so you can lay out your beads. I have to admit that I don't usually pay attention to the measurements, but I love the ridges so I can line up beads to see how they look against one another. Bead mats are essentially placemats for your worktable. They keep beads from rolling away. I have a stack in different colors on my workbench at all times.

crochet hooks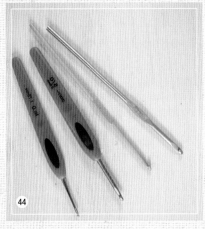

Small crochet hooks are necessary when crocheting a chain with or without beads. Crochet hooks range in price depending on whether they have a special ergonomic handle. When selecting a hook, I compare the scale of the cord to the actual hook to see whether it will be easy to catch the cord. An all-purpose solution or a good starting point is a size G (1 mm) hook.

butane torch, tweezers, soldering pad & quenching bowl

The only torch work in this book consists of balling up wires to make head pins, so all you'll need is a micro butane torch. They're cordless, which is my favorite thing about them safety-wise. You can pick them up at a large hardware store or online. You'll also need a heat-safe ceramic pad to work over, and tweezers to hold on to the hot metal. You can pick up ceramic pads or firebrick at fireplace supply shops or at special jewelry-making supply companies online. A bowl (made of heat-tempered glass such as Pyrex) filled with water will work as a quenching bowl to cool your metal after heating.

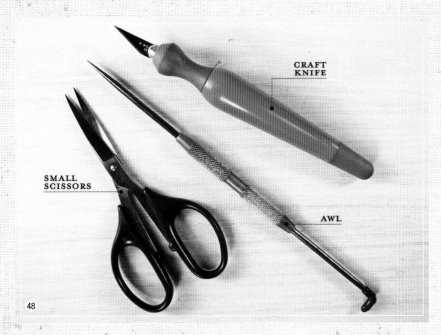

SMALL
SCISSORS

CRAFT
KNIFE

AWL

48

49

If you prefer not to work with a butane torch you can just buy premade balled head pins.

pearl knotter 46

The whole point of knotting is to avoid the beads rubbing against each other and getting damaged. A pearl knotter isn't just for knotting pearls. You can knot gemstones and other delicate beads as well. I started out knotting by hand, but now you can get a fancy tool to aid in the process. It takes a little practice to build up speed.

coiling tool 47

You can make perfect wire coils by wrapping wire around a mandrel. Coiling tools come with mandrels in different sizes, so you can make coils in various diameters.

bench block & hammer

A bench block is a tempered steel block for supporting metal while hammering. I keep mine within reach on my work-table because it's one of my most-used tools.

There are hammers from the hardware store and then there are special jewelry hammers. The difference is the jewelry hammers have highly polished surfaces, so when you hammer your metal, the hammer won't leave a texture on the surface. A chasing hammer is used throughout this book. The chasing hammer's head has a large flat side and a round side. You can also purchase a straight-edged hammer to create a linear texture.

miscellaneous tools 48

You may need small sharp scissors, a craft knife, a wood-burning tool, third-hand tweezers, and an awl. Small scissors are useful for clipping threads

and ribbons. A craft knife is necessary if you plan on cutting leather. Make custom designs on wooden beads with a wood-burning tool. There are many tips that make different patterns. A third-hand is a jeweler's tool consisting of a weighted base that holds a pair of reverse-action tweezers; it can hold your work, leaving you with both hands free. Use an awl to poke holes in felt beads or push fabric into the center of beads.

brass brush 49

If you use liver of sulfur, you won't regret getting a brass brush. A brass brush is just what it sounds like—a brush with soft brass bristles. Use it along with a couple of drops of dishwashing soap and water to add a gentle shine to your metal or to burnish over a liver of sulfur patina.

techniques

This chapter gives you all the information you'll need for successful necklaceology.

working with stringing materials

Stringing materials are the foundation for your pieces. The weight, adaptability, and aesthetics of the beads are just a few things to consider when constructing a piece. Experiment with the following techniques and let your designs come together.

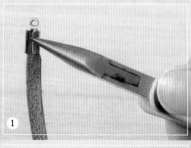

adding a bead stopper

Pinch the two ends of the coil between your fingers to open the spring. Put the wire in between the coils and release the ends, making it stay snug on the wire.

finishing the ends of cords

Use chain-nose pliers to attach fold-over findings. Roll one side over **1** and then roll over the opposite side **2**. Place the pliers over the entire finding and squeeze to flatten securely **3**. If the finding is easily marred, put a piece of masking tape or two on the inside jaws of your pliers to protect it.

knotting

I was so intimidated by knotting before writing this book. Why? I have no idea—this is really pretty easy to do! I definitely think practice makes perfect, but we all have to start somewhere. I've tried to make this as simple as possible for us beginners.

1 Start with a length of silk thread that has a needle attached. Tie the non-needle end onto a jump ring and leave a 1-inch (2.5 cm) tail. String a large-holed bead over both ends and tie another knot **4**. String three or four beads onto the cord **5**.

2 Pick up a pearl knotter (page 21) with your right hand. Slide one bead up against the jump ring end. Pull the jump

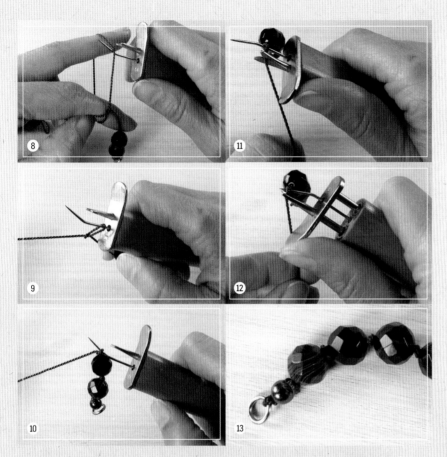

crocheting a chain

Select the cord or yarn you want to use. Make a slipknot, and secure it to the crochet hook ⓲. Use the hook to pull the long end of the cord through the loop on the crochet hook ⓯, dropping the last loop from the hook to create a chain. This is called chain stitch. Continue in the same manner for the desired length ⓰. When you reach the end, cut the long end of the yarn, leaving a tail 2 or 3 inches (5.1 or 7.6 cm) long. Pull this tail through the last loop on the crochet hook to secure.

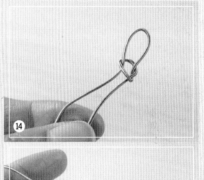

ring end of the cord through the ring finger and middle finger on your left hand, then pull toward you and up over your index finger (making it so the jump ring end wraps away from you) ❻.

3 Take the jump ring end up next to your index finger and drop the end through the hole ❼. Poke the awl-looking part on the knotting tool into the center of the loop ❽ and transfer the loop over to the knotting tool.

4 The jump ring end can now be in your right hand as your left hand pulls the long tail ❾, sliding the knot up against the first bead ❿. But wait, that's not all! Turn the knotting tool

around (as seen in the photo) and position the cord in the little V slot ⓫. Pull the left tail and push up on the lever to slide the knot up against the bead ⓬. Pretty neat, huh?

5 Repeat knotting and stringing to the desired length ⓭. When you come to the last bead, string another large-holed bead and a jump ring. Knot by hand next to the jump ring and then thread the needle through the large-holed bead and create another knot. Trim the end. Secure each of the end knots with a touch of adhesive.

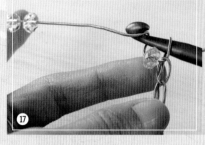

crocheting a chain with beads

Crocheting a beaded chain isn't difficult once you've mastered the basic chain stitch. Before doing anything else, thread the desired number of beads onto the cord. (You may need to use a collapsible needle (page 19) for this step depending on how small the holes are in the beads.) Again, secure the cord to the crochet hook with a slipknot. Chain the desired number, then slide a bead up next to the crochet hook and pull the long tail through the loop on the crochet hook, locking the bead in place **17**. Make another chain stitch with or without a bead and continue onward **18**.

making connections

Jewelry making is all about connections. Crimping, linking, wrapping, and riveting are just some of the ways to assemble adornments. I have my favorites, and I think you will, too!

crimping

There are three ways that I secure beading wire to a jump ring or other finding. For me, which method I choose for any given necklace comes down to functionality versus aesthetics.

Traditional Crimping

For a really secure connection, you can fold over the crimp beads. You'll need the special crimping pliers for this (page 19). Do *not* trim away excess wire until you're satisfied with the crimp. Start by spreading the wires apart and placing the crimp tube or bead in the

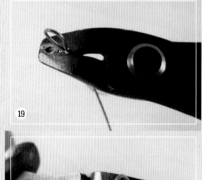

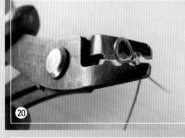

U-shaped section of the pliers; crimp down so that a wire is on each side of the U **19**. Turn the bead 90°, place it in the next opening in the pliers, and crimp down—this process rolls or folds the bead over **20**. If the crimp bead cracks, try to snip it away from the wire with wire cutters and start again. If it's really bad, you may have to re-string (all my sympathy if this happens—I've been there, too!). You can hide the crimp beads with special crimp bead covers. Use chain-nose pliers to close the crimp cover **21**.

Flat Crimping

You can use chain-nose pliers to flatten a crimp bead, making it into a rectangle or square shape **22**. I like this method for lightweight strands. You can also separate beads along a strand of wire and create space between them by crimping. Sometimes, for heavier strands, I double the crimp beads for added security.

Scrimps

Lastly, you can use Scrimp findings. Run the beading wire just as you would through a traditional crimp bead. Use the tiny screwdriver that comes with the Scrimp findings to tighten it, securing the wire **23**. Scrimps come in different sizes depending on the diameter of your beading wire.

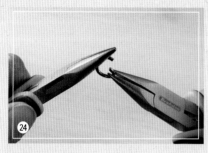

opening & closing
a jump ring

It's impossible to form a ring back into a circle if it's been pried open. You need to twist your jump rings open from side to side; conversely, once your pieces are connected, twist them closed. So here's the methodology: Place the ends of two chain-nosed pliers at either side of the opening in the jump ring and twist open . Repeat to close. If the ring won't close, open it a little, force the two ends past the point of center just a little, and then twist it back closed. This creates a pressure fit.

using mini bolts

I find mini nuts and bolts addictive (see Watchworks, page 70)! They're a little tricky to use because of their size, but they're so wonderful because they create instant interest. You can find them at specialty jewelry supply companies online and sometimes at hobby or train shops. Be sure to purchase a tiny screwdriver and/or wrench set, too. It's a must when working with these tiny pieces.

1 To use, drill or punch a small hole in your materials (see page 27).

2 From the front or back, thread the bolt through all the layers, then connect a mini washer and a nut ㉕. With heavy-duty wire cutters, cut off

the excess bolt just above the nut, leaving just enough for a rivet ㉖. Tap the end with a chasing hammer on a steel bench block. This makes it so the bolt can't accidentally unscrew and come apart ㉗.

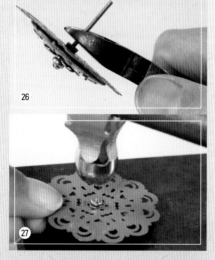

THE TOP OF THE COMPONENT
AFTER MINI-BOLTING IT TOGETHER.

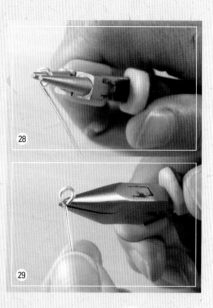

working
with wire

Making loops on the end of wires is one of the most common jewelry-making skills you'll need. I use loops to create beaded links, dangles, and even clasps. A word to beginners: everyone's loops look scary at first. Please don't be too critical of your first or thirtieth attempts. Deal?

making simple loops

Simple loops are useful for making links and connections. Grasp the end of the wire with your round-nose pliers and roll the wire around until it meets ㉘. Use your chain-nose pliers to straighten the loop by grasping the back base of the loop and making a slight turn ㉙. This should align it with the rest of the wire.

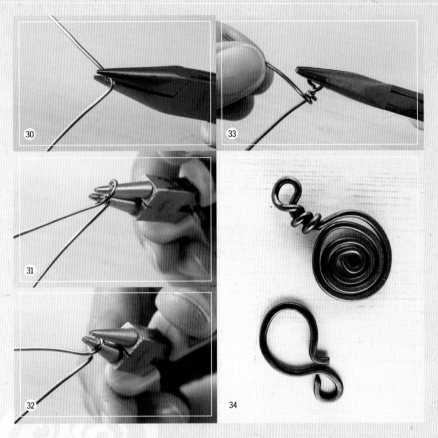

Continue coiling until you reach the desired length ㉟. This piece can be strung as is or chopped into smaller coil beads ㊱.

making balled head pins

Copper, sterling silver, and fine silver wires can all be balled on the end to make head pins. Why make your own when you can buy them? With commercial head pins, you just have to settle for whatever length you can find. Make them, and you also control the size of the balls on the ends.

1 Cut a length of wire. Hold the wire with tweezers above your soldering pad. Position the hottest part of the torch's flame, which is the tip of the dark blue section, at the end of the wire.

2 Gently heat ㊲ just above the end of the wire—the wire should zip up into the beginning of a ball shape. Slowly move your flame around in a tight circle and move upward. The tiny ball will follow the heat upward and grow in size ㊳. If you're balling up larger gauge wires, like 16-gauge, you may need to place a piece of heat-safe block behind the wire to keep the heat contained.

3 Quench the wire by dropping it in a bowl filled with water.

making wrapped loops

Wrapped loops started out being my least favorite thing to do in jewelry making and now this technique is my favorite. Funny how that happens. I love how secure they are and the decorative element the wrapped section adds. You can make perfect wraps or messy ones.

Make a 90° bend 1 to 1½ inches (2.5 to 3.8 cm) in from the end of the wire ㉚. Grasp the wire in the bent section using round-nose pliers. Wrap the wire up and around the top of the pliers, ending on the side of the pliers ㉛. Remove the pliers, put the bottom jaw into the loop, and wrap the wire underneath to complete the circle ㉜. Switch to chain-nose pliers and grasp the loop. Use your fingers to wrap the extra wire around the main wire ㉝. Trim at the desired length of coil. ㉞ shows a clasp and dangle you can make with simple and wrapped loops.

coiling wire

Clamp the base of the coiling tool to a table. The coiling tool comes with mandrels in different diameters. Select the diameter you want and place it in the corresponding hole on the base piece. Wrap the wire around the mandrel and simply begin turning.

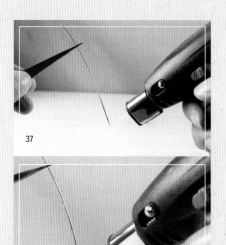

37

38

42

43

Then, working in a properly ventilated area, mix the solution according to the manufacturer's instructions. You can either simply drop your metal piece in the container or hold it with tweezers and dip it until the desired color is achieved. A fresh batch of liver of sulfur will work much faster than one that's been sitting for a day. It's a good idea to have a bowl of cold water sitting next to the solution so you can rinse your piece off quickly once you're happy with the effect. Give the piece a final rinse in cold soapy water. Completely oxidized surfaces will turn chalky and eventually flake off. To prevent this from happening, brush with

a brass brush (page 21) and a few drops of dishwashing soap **40**. Use pumice powder (page 18) and a touch of water to remove oxidation from the high spots **41**. Brass brushing is your last step after pumicing to brighten your metal. Apply a drop of dish soap to the brush bristles and brush over your piece.

applying finishes

When you start making jewelry, you'll find that there are thousands of components available for your creations. Some are perfect as is and some may benefit from a little tweaking. You can add stunning finishes to commercial components in a few simple ways.

liver of sulfur

You can intentionally oxidize your metal pieces with liver of sulfur, a magical though smelly solution. It comes in gel or rock form. Use liver of sulfur on silver for a very durable patina that can range in color from gold all the way to black. Copper turns more brownish, then black, while brass goes brown. Essentially, the longer you leave the metal in the solution, the darker the finish **39**.

The process is easy. First make sure the metal is free of dirt and oil, or the liver of sulfur won't take to the surface.

39

40

41

paint

Spray paints are easy to use, but make sure to work in a ventilated space. I love painting filigree pieces and then sanding them in a circular pattern, removing paint and adding texture. My favorite way to apply brush-on enamels is with a paintbrush. Just dip the end of the brush in the paint and make dots wherever you like **42**. Of course, you can always brush the paint on, too.

Check out **43**. On the left I used the end of the paintbrush to create dots, and on the right I rubbed a glob of paint over the top of the flower so the paint sunk into the recessed areas.

Metal spray paints and brush-on enamel paints are a fast and exciting way to add color to your metal and glass pieces. Check out the hobby and craft shops for enamel paints and mini cans of spray paint used for model painting. Filigree pieces, pendants, and metal beads are all good candidates for painting, adding yet another handmade element to your work.

alcohol inks

Alcohol inks can be used singly or in multiples to create layers. Apply a drop of ink to a scrap of commercial felt and then rub it over your metal piece ④④. Add a second or third color if you wish ④⑤. You can remove color with a special remover sold alongside the inks or sand it away with sandpaper. It never hurts to experiment on scrap pieces of metal to see what effects you can get by mixing colors.

texturing

Texturing is something I use on almost all of my necklaces. It's just another layer that adds visual interest to the elements of your design. Oftentimes I alter commercial findings such as daisy spacers, filigree pieces, and bead bars by sanding or hammering to add a handmade element.

Sanding

Sandpaper is always within reach on my worktable. I scuff anything and everything from super shiny silver clasps to a pendant that has a brass plating on it. I generally use 220-grit sandpaper because of its all-purpose nature. You can opt for a circular motion, back and forth, or all over the place. If you're uncertain, practice on a scrap surface first.

Hammering

Another favorite texture tool is the chasing hammer (page 19). As I mentioned before, I hammer a lot of commercial findings. I'm not saying it always works out, but 95% of the time I like the effect. If you're opting for a hammered texture, support your piece on a steel bench block while you hammer ④⑥. Without support, the metal will take the shape of whatever's under it. One time I dented a wood table because I forgot to put the bench block under my metal! If you'd like, you can put a dish towel under your block to dull the hammering sound and help protect your work surface. This flower looks dramatically different after hammering ④⑦.

wood-burning tool

Find a scrap piece of wood to practice your design on first. (This is also useful

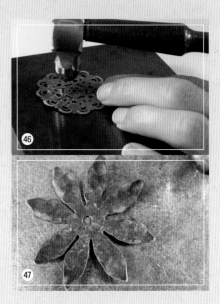

for making sure the tool is hot before working on your actual beads.) Screw the desired attachment tip into the end of the wood-burning tool. Allow the tool to heat up and test on a scrap surface to see the effect. Working in a well-ventilated area, touch the tip of the tool to painted or plain wooden beads to apply the design ④⑧.

49

making holes

Knowing how to drill holes in various elements **49** can make incorporating diverse materials, such as found objects, that much easier.

using a hole punch

It's so easy to punch holes in metal. You can also use the punches to enlarge holes already in metal elements such as bead caps. Some punches look like paper hole punches and others are larger with interchangeable taps and dies so you can vary the size of hole you want. They both work the same. To use, simply mark your metal with a permanent marker, put the punch on top of the marking, and squeeze down on the handle until you hear it "punch" through. The larger hand punch is great for going through thick metal such as coins **50**.

50

using a drill

You may need to use a handheld drill when making holes in thicker materials. For wood and plastic, simply mark your hole and drill. For metal, mark your hole placement with a pen, place the tip of a center punch on it, and hammer the tool **51**. This makes a divot in the metal so your drill bit has a seat, preventing it from skidding around on the metal when you start drilling **52**. After you drill the hole, you may need to use a needle file to remove the burr or smooth any rough edges.

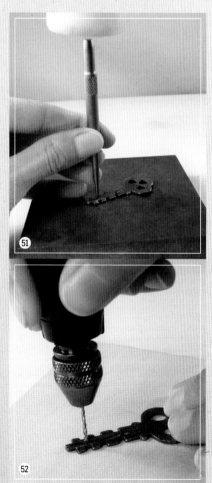

51

52

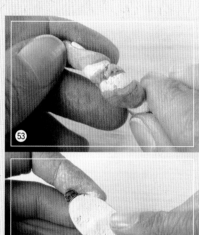

53

54

55

working with epoxy clay

Follow the manufacturer's instructions for the epoxy clay. Mix equal amounts of part A and B of the epoxy clays together **53**. Roll them into a ball **54** and fill the bezel frame. Push embellishments into the clay, then let dry **55**.

rococo ribbon

The eighteenth-century style of art known as rococo is notorious for its glorious excess: elaborate ornamentation, profusions of foliage and scrollwork, and plentiful gold leaf. It originated in France. In paintings of the period, women wear ribbon chokers with a jewel at the throat. Toned down, the style serves as the inspiration for this necklace.

COLLECT

5 square double-sided
  slider beads,
  17 x 17 mm

2 flat-back crystals,
  4 mm

3 vintage black glass
  buttons, 13 mm

Black glass flower but-
  ton, 7 mm (optional)

15 inches (38 cm)
  of 1-inch-wide
  (2.5 cm) aqua and
  black ribbon

1½ inches (3.8 cm) of
  silver chain, 5 mm

2 gunmetal ribbon end
  findings, 21 x 6 mm

Silver lobster clasp,
  10 mm

3 silver jump rings,
  5 mm

320-grit sandpaper
  (optional)

Liver of sulfur solution

Multipurpose epoxy

INSTRUMENTS

Toothpick
Clothespins
Chain-nose pliers

TECHNIQUES

Adding patina

DIMENSIONS

15.5 inches (39.4 cm)
  long

methodology

1 If you wish, you can scuff the square beads a bit with sand-paper to remove the shine and then apply a liver of sulfur patina. These beads are double-sided—recessed on one side and decorative on the other (FIG. 01).

FIG.01

2 String the five square beads onto the ribbon so that the first one has the recessed area fac-ing up, the next has the decorative side facing up, and so on.

3 Use a toothpick to apply a dot of adhesive to the center of the decorative pattern on the beads and then place a flat-back crystal on top (FIG. 02).

FIG.02

4 Apply adhesive to the back of the 13-mm buttons and place one in the recessed area of the beads (FIG. 03). Clamp in place with clothespins until dry.

ANALYZE
THE DATA
The ribbon has to be wider than the sliders. Otherwise, the sliders will skate along the strand.

FIG.03

5 Attach the ribbon end find-ings to the ends of the ribbon. Crimp them in place with chain-nose pliers. Attach the lobster clasp to one end of the necklace with a 5-mm jump ring. Attach the chain to the other side with one 5-mm jump ring. If you wish, embellish the clasp with a flower button at-tached to the end of the chain with a 5-mm jump ring (FIG. 04).

FIG.04

COLLECT

- Crystals and beads to fill watch finding*
- 26 three-cut red Czech glass beads, 5 x 7 mm
- 3 yards (2.7 m) of 26-gauge silver wire (optional, for nest)
- 1 yard (91.4 cm) of 20-gauge silver wire
- Pocket watch finding, 38 mm
- Two 18-gauge silver jump rings, 6 mm
- One 20-gauge silver jump ring, 4 mm
- Pewter clasp, 20 mm
- Alcohol ink
- 120-grit sandpaper

* I used a wire nest, a crystal heart, and three 5-mm beads.

INSTRUMENTS

- Miniature screwdriver
- Small paintbrush
- Wire cutters
- Round-nose pliers
- Needle-nose pliers
- Chain-nose pliers
- Measuring tape

TECHNIQUES

- Alcohol inks
- Wrapped loop
- Opening and closing a jump ring

DIMENSIONS

16 inches (40.6cm)

I'm always thinking about symbolism. With their reflective qualities and clarity, crystals are a powerful symbol for light. This necklace houses tiny crystals and thus creates a special reminder to always look for the light.

chronos

methodology

1 Remove the back from the pocket watch finding with a miniature screwdriver. Apply a coat or two of alcohol ink to it, and allow to dry. Sand to remove some of the color and create texture (FIG. 01).

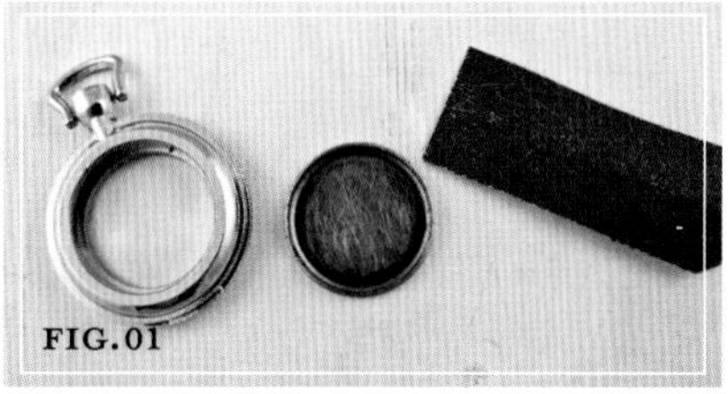

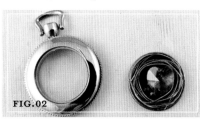

FIG.01

2 Fill the finding with a wire nest using the 26-gauge wire, a crystal heart, and small beads (FIG. 02), and replace the back.

FIG.02

FIG.03

3 To create a beaded chain, make a wrapped bead link with the red beads and the 20-gauge wire (FIG. 03).

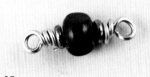

FIG.04

4 Create a second link, but before closing one end, hook the first link into it before wrapping (FIG. 04).

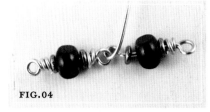

sketchbook

EXPERIMENT

You can streamline the look and spend less time making this necklace by using commercial chain. I love the simplicity this creates, changing the focus so it's entirely on the pendant.

FIG.05

5 Create two sections of chain that are 7 inches (17.8 cm) long and one section that is 2¾ inches (7 cm) long. The loop that connects the 7-inch (17.8 cm) pieces to the 2¾-inch (7 cm) piece can be slightly larger than the rest (FIG. 05).

FIG.07

6 Connect the watch finding to the 2¾-inch (7 cm) piece of chain with a 6-mm jump ring (FIG. 06).

7 Attach the clasp to the chain. Attach the loop end of the clasp with a 6-mm jump ring and the toggle end with the 4-mm jump ring (FIG. 07).

FIG.06

These beads were
too bright on their own,
so I put a haze of silver
WireLace netting over
them to tone down
the color a bit. The
wire-wrapped beads are
so fun to make; this is
a festive piece all the
way around!

it's a wrap

COLLECT

21 multicolored dyed
    agate beads, 12 mm
2 silver spacer beads,
    4 mm
4 yards (3.6 m) of
    18-gauge silver wire
24 inches (61 cm) of
    WireLace ribbon in
    titanium, 12 mm
24 inches (61 cm) of
    49-strand .018-inch
    (.46 mm) beading
    wire
4 silver crimp beads
Barrel clasp, 15 x 15 mm
Multipurpose adhesive

INSTRUMENTS

Mandrel, 3.4 mm
Wire cutters
Crimping pliers
Chain-nose pliers
Coiling tool
Needle

TECHNIQUES

Coiling
Crimping

DIMENSIONS

16.5 inches (41.9 cm)

methodology
create the wire beads

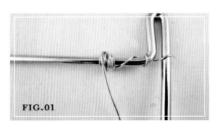

FIG.01

Using the coiling tool and 18-gauge
wire, wrap the wire around the
mandrel (FIG. 01). The messier, the
better. Stop at the desired diameter, which is
determined by
the beads you
are using. The
wire beads here
are slightly
smaller than
the diameter
of the agate
beads (FIG. 02).
Repeat to make
a total of 20
wire beads.

FIG.02

create the necklace

1 Drop one agate bead down into
the wire ribbon and make a
twist; leave an approximate 1¼-inch
(3.2 cm) tail for finishing the ends
(FIG. 03).

FIG.03

FIG.04

2 Make a twist at the end of the
wire ribbon and string a wire
bead (FIG. 04).

3 Untwist the ribbon and drop
another agate bead down into
the WireLace followed by a twist.
Continue alternating agate beads
and wire beads until you use up all
but two of the agate beads, ending
with the wire beads.

finish the ends

1 String a crimp bead onto
a 4-inch (10.2 cm) piece of
beading wire. Thread the two ends
through a silver spacer bead and an
agate bead (FIG. 05). Pull snug and
flatten the crimp bead.

FIG.05

2 Drop this bead down into the
lace so the wire pokes out the
end. Twist the WireLace around the
threading wire and trim, leaving
approximately ⅛ inch (3 mm).

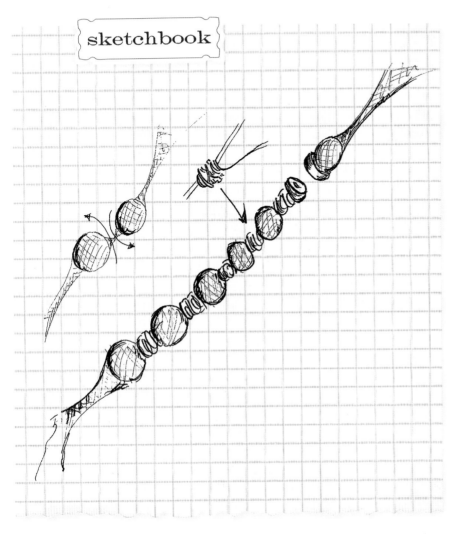

sketchbook

FIG.08

4 String a crimp bead onto the wire so it sits down in the clasp, and flatten it with chain-nose pliers. Trim the end of the wire so the magnet sits flat in the finding.

5 Apply a dot of adhesive to the magnet and inside of the clasp. I used a needle to pick up the magnet and slide it into the clasp (FIG. 08).

6 Repeat for the opposite side.

3 String the barrel clasp end onto the beading wire so the part where the magnet sits is at the opposite side of the bead (FIG. 06).

Apply a drop of adhesive and push the clasp up against the bead. Use a coil stopper to hold the clasp in place while it dries (FIG. 07).

FIG.06

FIG.07

kiss the bride

This easy pattern is a great spin on the classic pearl necklace. You don't have to be a bride, either—make one in any color of glass pearls and crystals.

1 Cut three pieces of beading wire 20 inches (50.8 cm) long. Secure them together using a bead stopper clamped 2 inches (5.1 cm) from the ends.

2 String a gold spacer bead over all three strands of wire. Now we will split the strands and string individually.

On strand 1, string a pearl, a crystal, and a pearl.

On strand 2, string a crystal, a pearl, and a crystal.

On strand 3, string a crystal, a pearl, and a crystal (FIG. 01). String another gold spacer over all three strands.

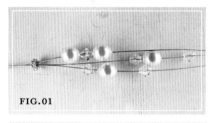

FIG.01

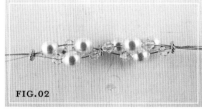

FIG.02

3 Repeat step 2 (FIG. 02).

4 Repeat step 2 again except instead of a gold spacer, string a glass pearl over all three strands.

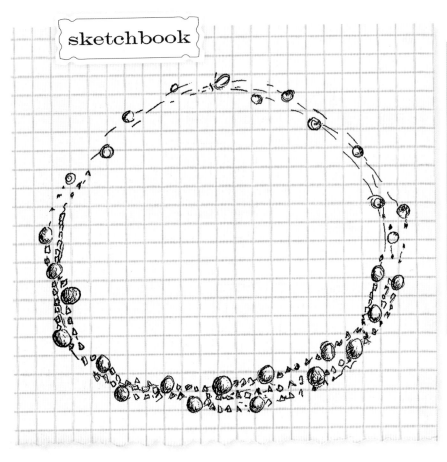

sketchbook

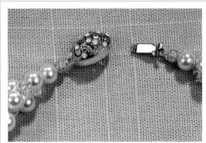

over all three wires and thread the wires through the clasp and back through the crimp bead. Crimp and repeat on the other side (FIG. 05).

FIG.06

5 Repeat step 4 (FIG. 03).

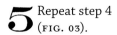

FIG.03

FIG.04

6 Continue stringing, alternating three sections separated by gold spacers and two sections separated by pearls, until you reach the end, ending with a gold spacer (FIG. 04).

7 Remove the stopper bead. String a pearl and crimp bead

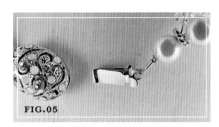

FIG.05

8 Finish by attaching the crimp bead covers over the crimp beads with chain-nose pliers (FIG. 06).

santa fe

Leather and turquoise are so evocative of the American southwest. Santa Fe is the second oldest city in the United States. The Spanish established it in 1607, although of course Native Americans had lived in the area for at least a thousand years before it became a town.

COLLECT

10 silver beads,
   2 x 5 mm
8 brown wooden beads,
   15 x 17 mm
2 turquoise beads,
   20 mm
22 inches (56 cm) of
   49-strand .018-inch
   (.46 mm) beading
   wire
5 inches (12.7 cm) of
   20-gauge silver wire
Strip of brown leather,
   1 x 15 inches (2.5
   x 38.1 x 2.5 cm)
Brown waxed linen
Liver of sulfur solution
   (optional)
Multipurpose adhesive

INSTRUMENTS

Wire cutters
Awl
Darning needle
Chain-nose pliers
Round-nose pliers
Craft knife

TECHNIQUES

Adding patina
Wrapped loop

DIMENSIONS

14.5 inches (36.8 cm)

sketchbook

methodology

If desired, apply a liver of sulfur patina to the silver beads to antique them a bit.

stitch the beads

1 String a silver bead and a wooden bead onto the beading wire. Repeat five more times, followed by a silver bead and a turquoise bead, then repeat the wooden bead pattern two times.

2 Place the row of beads on the leather. Use the adhesive to adhere the beads in a row where you want them to lie on the choker (FIG. 01).

FIG.01

3 Use the awl to poke two holes next to the last bead on each side so the beading wire can go down and back up to the top of the piece. Thread the extra beading wire back through a few of the beads on both sides (FIG. 02).

4 Poke holes on either side of the beads for the waxed linen stitches. Thread the needle with the

FIG.02

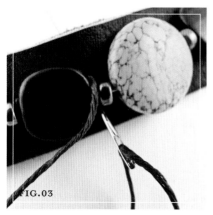

FIG.03

create the closure

1 Thread a 4-inch (10.2 cm) piece of silver wire through the remaining turquoise bead. Bring both ends down and to the middle on the back side. Use pliers to make a 90° bend and wrap the other wire around a few times. Make a loop with the bent wire and wrap the remaining tail up toward the coil. Trim away the excess (FIG. 05).

FIG.05

2 With a craft knife, cut a 1-inch (2.5 cm) slit in the leather ½ inch (1.3 cm) in from the edge (FIG. 06).

FIG.06

3 Stitch the turquoise button ¾ inch (1.9 cm) in from the edge (FIG. 07).

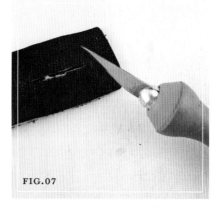

FIG.07

waxed linen. Starting at one end on the back side, bring the linen up to the front and make one stitch to cover the beading wire. Continue punching holes and stitching in between each bead (FIG. 03).

5 Tie the ends off on the back side (FIG. 04).

FIG.04

COLLECT

24 round faceted black beads, 4 mm

40 round faceted black beads, 6 mm

12 round faceted black beads, 8 mm

10 round faceted black beads, 10 mm

4 rhinestone rondelles, 6 mm

2 black glass beads, 15 mm

6 black and silver pressed-glass beads, 20 mm

18 black bicone beads, 4 x 3 mm

2 round faceted black beads, 5 x 8 mm

2 silver rhinestone beads, 6 mm

12 round Silver Shadow Swarovski crystals, 6 mm

36 inches (91.4 cm) of 49-strand .018-inch (.46 mm) silver beading wire

5 inches (12.7 cm) of 20-gauge silver wire

2 silver double loop end bars, 15 x 15 mm

4 silver crimp beads

Silver jump ring, 6 mm

Vintage glass button, 25 mm

INSTRUMENTS

Wire cutters
Crimping pliers
Round-nose pliers
Chain-nose pliers
Chasing hammer
Steel bench block

TECHNIQUES

Crimping
Simple loop
Hammering
Opening and closing a jump ring

DIMENSIONS

16.5 inches (41.9 cm) long

Invited to a wedding?
Cocktail party? Prom-bound?
Make this piece in any color
for a chic accessory.

grace

methodology
string the beads

STRAND #1
String one 4-mm glass bead, five 6-mm glass beads, six 8-mm glass beads, five 10-mm glass beads onto the beading wire (FIG. 01), a rhinestone rondelle, a 15-mm glass bead, a rhine-

FIG.01

FIG.02

stone rondelle, a black and silver bead, and a black bicone bead onto the beading wire. Repeat the black and silver bead alternating with the bicone bead four more times, then end with a black and silver bead (FIG. 02). String the other half of the necklace in the reverse order, starting with the rhinestone rondelle, so it mirrors the first half.

STRAND #2

String eleven 4-mm beads, fifteen 6-mm beads, one 5 x 8-mm black bead (FIG. 03), a silver rhinestone bead, a black bicone bead, and a crystal onto the beading wire. String 11 more crystals separated by the bicone beads, ending with a bicone (FIG. 04). String the other half of the necklace so it mirrors the first.

FIG.03

FIG.04

finish the ends

1 Secure the ends of the wire to the end bars so the longer strand is on the outer loops and the smaller strand is on the inner loops with crimp beads (FIG. 05).

FIG.05

2 Create a spiral at the end of the silver wire, wrapping it around to make a hook shape. Make a simple loop at the end of the wire, positing the loop so it's perpendicular to the spiral. Hammer the spiral flat on the bench block with your chasing hammer. Connect it to one end of the necklace (FIG. 06).

FIG.06

ANALYZE THE DATA

Staying with a monochromatic palette keeps this design elegant.

3 Use the silver jump ring to attach the button to the other end (FIG. 07).

FIG.07

ranch hand

I think carnelian and turquoise are simply made for each other. Lasso this piece around your neck for some Southwest style.

COLLECT

50 turquoise nuggets,
   4 x 3 mm
72 round turquoise
   beads, 2 mm
40 silver bead caps,
   5 mm
21 round orange glass
   beads, 5 mm
18 turquoise cube
   beads, 5 mm
9 square bead frames,
   8.5 mm
9 round orange glass
   beads, 3 mm
Southwest theme
   enamel pendant
4 yards (3.6 m) of
   26-gauge silver wire
20 inches (50.8 cm) of
   49-strand .018-inch
   (.46 mm) beading
   wire
2 silver crimp beads
Silver crimp bead cover
Toggle bar, 35 mm
1 silver lobster clasp,
   13 mm

INSTRUMENTS

Mandrel, 1.6 mm
Wire cutters
Crimping pliers
Chain-nose pliers

TECHNIQUES

Coiling
Crimping

DIMENSIONS

16 inches (40.6 cm)

methodology
create the beaded beads

1 String four turquoise nuggets and seven 2-mm turquoise beads in any order onto the silver wire. Coil them around the small mandrel (FIG. 01).

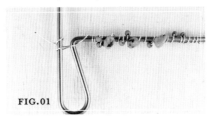

FIG.01

2 Cut the wire, leaving a little wire on either side of the coil (FIG. 02).

3 Stretch the coil out a little and fold in half (FIG. 03).

FIG.02

4 Twist, stretch, and fold again. There really is no method here—simply wad and twist it up (FIG. 04). Repeat to make 10 beads total.

FIG.03

FIG.04

string the necklace

1 String one crimp bead and 10 turquoise nuggets onto the beading wire. Thread the tail of wire back through the crimp bead to make a loop and crimp. Use chain-nose pliers to place the crimp bead cover over the crimp bead (FIG. 05).

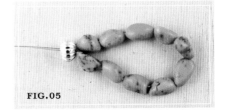

FIG.05

2 String on a silver bead cap, a 5-mm orange bead, a bead cap, a 2-mm turquoise bead, a beaded bead, a 2-mm turquoise bead, a silver bead cap, a 5-mm orange bead, a bead cap, a turquoise cube, a bead frame with a 3-mm orange bead in the center, and a turquoise cube onto the beading wire. Repeat this sequence eight more times (FIG. 06).

FIG.06

FIG.07

3 String a 2-mm turquoise bead, a beaded bead, a 2-mm turquoise bead, a bead cap, a 5-mm orange bead, and a bead cap onto the beading wire followed by a crimp bead and the toggle bar. Thread the wire back through the crimp bead, remove the slack, and crimp (FIG. 07).

pendant

String a 5-mm orange bead onto a piece of 20-gauge wire and finish with a wrapped loop on each end, attaching one end to the pendant and the other end to the lobster clasp before wrapping (FIG. 08). Clip the pendant onto the beaded loop as desired.

FIG.08

ANALYZE THE DATA

Since the pendant hooks on with a clasp, it's inter-changeable. You can wear this necklace without it, you can wear the necklace with a different pendant altogether, and you can even hang the pendant from other chains.

VARIATION

Change out pendants to suit your gear. Here's how to make a filigree stone pendant instead. You'll need the following:

Square filigree piece, 30 mm
Turquoise bead, 35 x 30 mm
Carnelian cabochon,
   10 x 6 mm
2 silver bead caps, 5 mm
1 round orange glass bead,
   5 mm

1 silver balled head pin
1 silver lobster clasp, 13 mm
Multipurpose glue

1 Glue the silver filigree piece to the top of the large turquoise bead and then glue the carnelian cabochon in the center (right).

2 String a bead cap, the large turquoise bead, a bead cap, and a 5-mm orange bead onto a balled head pin. Finish the end with a wrapped loop, attaching the lobster clasp before wrapping.

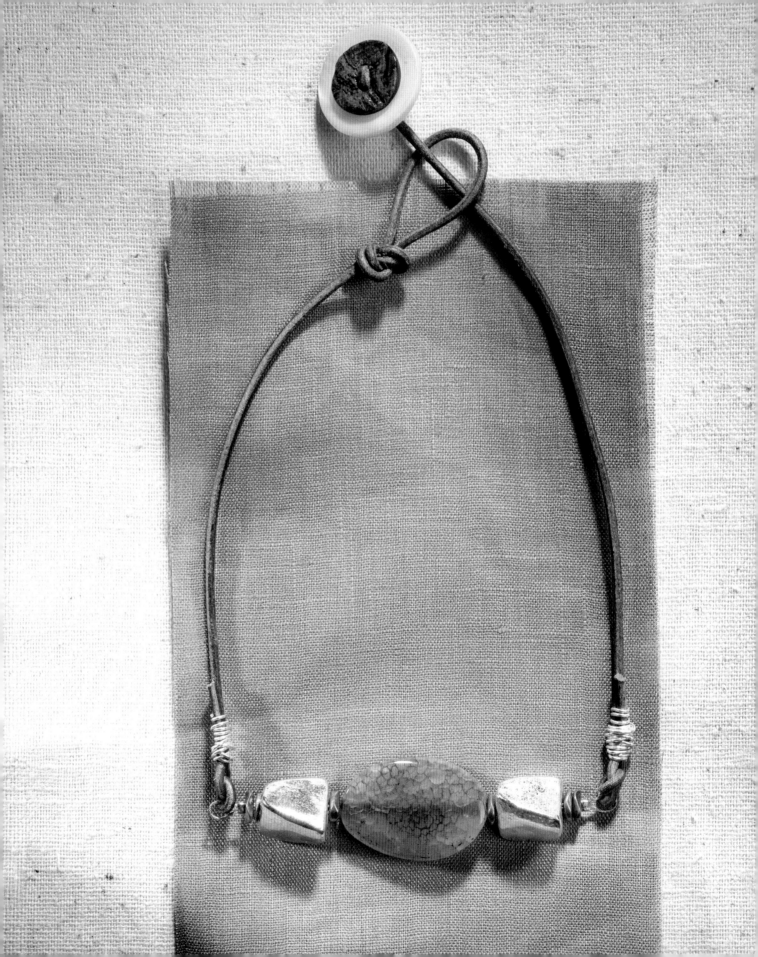

COLLECT

6 silver spacer beads, 4 mm

2 silver twist beads, 12 mm

Chunky purple dyed agate focal bead, 30 x 20 mm

Shell button, 20 mm

6 inches (15.2 cm) of 49-strand .024-inch (.61 mm) beading wire

20 inches (50.8 cm) of leather cord, 1 mm

6 inches (15.2 cm) of 26-gauge silver wire

2 crimp beads

220-grit sandpaper

Beeswax

INSTRUMENTS

Crimping pliers

Scissors

Wire cutters

TECHNIQUES

Crimping

DIMENSIONS

16.5 inches (41.9 cm) long

Jeans.
Plain white T.
Cowboy boots.
This necklace.
Done.

simple

methodology

1 Make a loop at one end of the beading wire and secure with a crimp bead (FIG. 01).

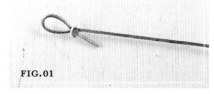

FIG.01

2 String two silver spacers, one silver twist bead, one silver spacer and the purple focal bead onto the beading wire. Repeat the silver bead sequence on the other side, pull taut, and finish the oppo-

FIG.02

site end with a loop, securing with a crimp bead (FIG. 02).

3 If desired, give the leather a rugged look by running it through a piece of sandpaper two or three times (FIG. 03). Smooth the leather again by running it through a piece of beeswax (FIG. 04).

FIG.03

FIG.04

4 Before you go cutting, take note that the measurements given here are approximate; it's easy to make your necklace longer or shorter. Cut the piece of leather in half. String the leather through the loop next to the beads and tie in a knot, leaving a short, ¾-inch (1.9 cm) tail. Wrap 1 to 2 inches (2.5 to 5.1 cm) of the silver wire around both pieces of leather next to the knot (FIG. 05). Repeat for the opposite side.

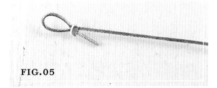

FIG.05

5 Fold over the end of the leather 1¾ inches (4.4 cm) from the end and make a loop with a knot. Thread the cord up through the back of the button and down through the opposite hole. Check the sizing and make a knot where you want the button to sit (FIG. 06).

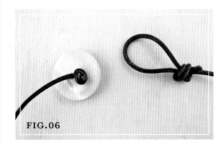

FIG.06

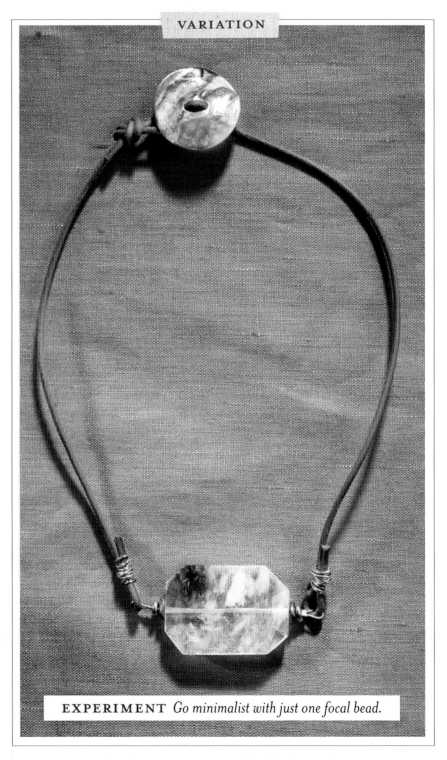

VARIATION

EXPERIMENT *Go minimalist with just one focal bead.*

COPPER
29
Cu
63.546

The Romans mined copper on Cyprus, leading to its Latin name of *cyprium*, which was later shortened to *cuprum*. That's why copper is abbreviated as Cu on the periodic table of elements. A double-channel finding is a great way to show off a favorite button.

see you

COLLECT

19 round copper beads, 3 mm

11 faceted brown glass beads, 4 mm

11 faceted Czech copper-coated beads, 4 mm

2 vintage buttons with shanks, 12 mm and 20 mm

Approximately 96 assorted beads, 3–8 mm (I used Czech fire-polished beads with copper and bronze coatings)

6 inches (15.2 cm) of clear nylon cord

20 inches (50.8 cm) of copper WireLace, 1 mm

20 inches (50.8 cm) of cocoa WireLace, 1 mm

20 inches (50.8 cm) of chocolate WireLace, 1 mm

20 inches (50.8 cm) of 18-gauge copper wire

Base metal silver-plated double-channel finding, 35 mm

Silver head pin, 2 inches (5.1 cm)

18-gauge copper jump ring, 6 mm

2 copper jump rings, 6 mm

Silver-plated clamshell end findings, 7 mm

Multipurpose epoxy with precision tip

Liver of sulfur (optional)

INSTRUMENTS

Collapsible beading needle
Chain-nose pliers
Round-nose pliers
Chasing hammer
Steel bench block

TECHNIQUES

Opening and closing a jump ring
Wrapped loop
Hammering
Adding patina

DIMENSIONS

17 inches (43.2 cm) long

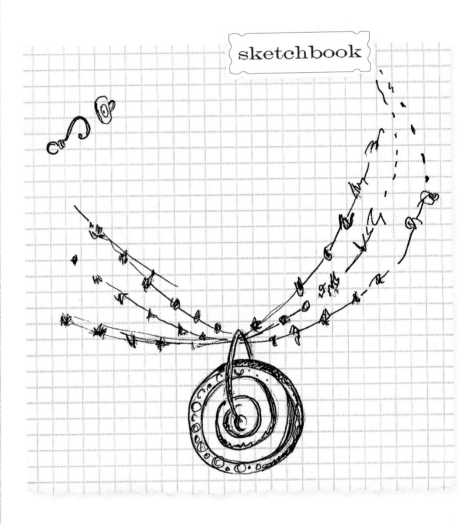

sketchbook

methodology
create the pendant

1 String 19 copper beads onto the nylon cord and tie the two ends in a knot to form a ring.

2 Thread the collapsible beading needle with one of the WireLace strands. String a 4-mm brown bead and a 4-mm copper-coated Czech bead onto the Wire-Lace. Repeat 10 more times for a total of 22 beads. Thread the needle through the first bead, apply a drop

FIG. 01

of adhesive on either side, and pull the ends snug (FIG. 01).

3 Apply a ring of adhesive to both channels of the channel finding and set the copper bead

FIG.02

ring in the inside ring and the Czech bead ring in the outer ring.

4 Thread a head pin through the inside ring of the channel finding and out through the top (FIG. 02). Finish the end of the wire with a wrapped loop.

5 Apply adhesive to the back side of the 20-mm button and set this piece on top of the ring of copper beads (FIG. 03).

FIG.03

string the necklace

1 Thread the collapsible beading needle with one WireLace color. String an assortment of approximately 32 beads onto the WireLace. You can opt for a pattern or string randomly. Repeat with the other two pieces of WireLace. Leave ¾ inch (1.9 cm) free in the center of the three strands (this is where the pendant will hang).

2 Position the beads the way you want them on the strands. Starting at one end of a strand, slide

a bead off to the side, apply a dot of adhesive on the WireLace, and slide the bead back into place. Repeat for each bead, then repeat for the remaining two strands. Let dry.

3 Attach the pendant to the center of the strands with the 18-gauge copper jump ring (FIG. 04).

FIG.04

FIG.05

finish the ends

1 Knot the three ends together and place a clamshell finding over the top (FIG. 05). Repeat on the other side.

2 Using round-nose pliers, make a hook with a wrapped loop from the copper wire. Hammer the hook flat on a steel bench block with a chasing hammer (FIG. 06).

FIG.06

FIG.07

If desired, apply a liver of sulfur patina to the hook.

3 Attach the hook to the loop on the clamshell finding with a 6-mm jump ring. Attach the button to the other clamshell loop with a 6-mm jump ring (FIG. 07).

COLLECT

41 round jasper beads, 5 mm

20 silver spacer beads, 5 mm

8 brown glass spacer beads, 6 mm

8 copper spacer beads, 6 mm

4 faceted carnelian beads, 14 x 10 mm

2 silver decorative spacer beads, 5 mm

Jasper pendant, 48 x 35 mm

Brass dragonfly charm, 50 x 39 mm

18 inches (45.7 cm) of brown suede, ⅛ inch (3 mm) wide

16 inches (40.6 cm) of base metal chain, 9 mm

5 inches (12.7 cm) of brass chain, 6.5 x 9.5 mm

1 yard (91.4 cm) of 49-strand .018-inch (.46 mm) beading wire

2 base metal jump rings, 8 mm

2 silver base metal jump rings, 5 mm

Base metal lobster clasp and loop, 15 mm

9 copper crimp beads, #1

INSTRUMENTS

Awl

Scissors

Tape measure

Crimping pliers

Wire cutters

Chain-nose pliers

TECHNIQUES

Crimping

Opening and closing a jump ring

DIMENSIONS

19 inches (48.3 cm) long

A walk around the pond—
the breeze blows, the
goldenrod sways, and the
dragonflies flit.

dragonfly

methodology
create the double necklace

1 Weave the suede in and out of the base metal chain, from end to end (FIG. 01). Use an awl to poke a hole into both ends of the leather. Using the 8-mm jump rings, attach the clasp to both the chain and the hole in the leather (FIG. 02).

FIG.01

FIG.02

2 String on two round jasper beads, a silver spacer, a glass spacer, a silver spacer, two jasper beads, a copper spacer, a carnelian bead, a copper spacer, two jasper beads, a silver spacer, a glass bead, a silver spacer, and two jasper beads onto the beading wire. Using crimp beads and crimping pliers, secure one end of the wire to a 5-mm jump ring and the opposite end to a single link of brass chain (FIG. 03).

FIG.03

sketchbook

2 Loop the wires around the chains and thread one end of the wire through the crimp bead. Pull both ends of the wire to remove the slack and crimp (FIG. 06).

FIG.06

FIG.04

3 Split the remaining brass chain into a section that is 10 links long. Repeat step 2, except this time attach the single link of brass chain from step 2 to one end of the wire, and the 10-link section to the opposite end (FIG. 04). Set aside.

4 Repeat steps 2 and 3.

5 Attach a 5-mm jump ring (from step 2) to the seventh link (counting from the clasp) on the base metal chain. Repeat for the second element made in step 4.

attach the pendant

1 String on one crimp bead, a round jasper bead, a silver spacer, a decorative spacer, the jasper pendant, the dragonfly pendant, a decorative spacer, two jasper beads, a silver spacer, two jasper beads, one silver spacer, two jasper beads, a silver spacer, and two jasper beads onto the beading wire (FIG. 05).

FIG.05

EXPERIMENT

The brown color of the suede threaded through the chain lends a subtle texture, but you could amp things up by using suede in a bright shade.

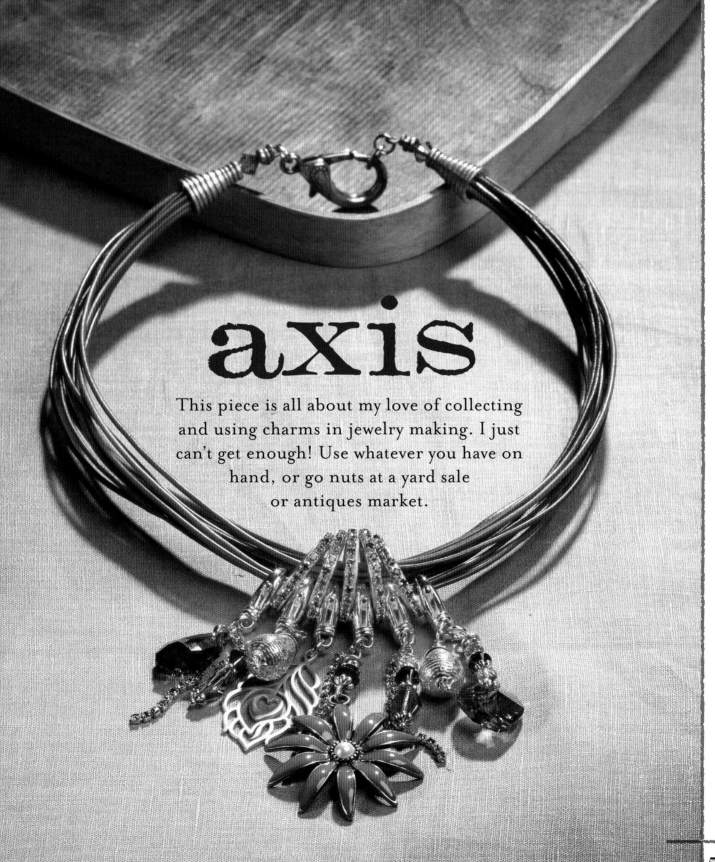

axis

This piece is all about my love of collecting
and using charms in jewelry making. I just
can't get enough! Use whatever you have on
hand, or go nuts at a yard sale
or antiques market.

COLLECT

6 bicone Padparadscha
    Swarovski crystals, 6 mm
Orange flower pendant,
    40 mm
Peacock feather pendant
Padparadscha Swarovski
    crystal heart, 16 mm
Fuchsia Swarovski crystal
    pendant, 15 x 21 mm
4 brass spacer beads, 5 mm
2 brass bead cones,
    16 x 11 mm
8 inches (20.3 cm) of
    Swarovski crystal cup
    chain in Fuchsia/Padpar-
    adscha, 2 mm
4 feet (1.2 m) of orange
    Greek leather
4 feet (1.2 m) of fuchsia
    Greek leather
4 feet (1.2 m) of red Greek
    leather
5 brass closed rings, 19 mm
2 brass jump rings
6 brass balled head pins
2 brass 20-gauge balled head
    pins
6 brass lobster clasps,
    18 x 12 mm
Brass lobster clasp,
    30 x 13 mm
Cup chain end findings
    with loop
Multipurpose adhesive

INSTRUMENTS

Clothespins
Wire cutters
Round-nose pliers
Chain-nose pliers
Scissors

TECHNIQUES

Wrapped loop
Opening and closing
    a jump ring

DIMENSIONS

18.5 inches (47 cm) long

methodology
make the rings

1 Embellish the five plain brass rings with crystal chain. Glue one end of the chain to the ring with multipurpose adhesive. Use a clothespin to hold it in place while it dries.

2 Wrap the chain around to meet where you started and cut to size. Apply a bead of adhesive around the ring and attach the chain. Use a clothespin to hold

FIG.01

the end of the chain in place while it dries (FIG. 01). Repeat for the remaining four rings.

VARIATION

EXPERIMENT
If you prefer, you can wear the necklace without the dangles.

make the dangles

To make the dangles seen here, I used anything from vintage earrings and crystal shapes to a pendant I found for $1.99. (In the Collect list, they're listed as a peacock feather pendant, a crystal heart, and a crystal pendant.) Make six dangles using the brass balled head pins to string crystals or whatever you like. Attach each dangle to a small lobster-claw clasp so they can be removed and added as desired. Here are a few ideas:

1 Attach cup end findings to extra rhinestone chain pieces (FIG. 02).

2 String crystals and brass spacer beads onto balled head pins and finish with a wrapped loop (FIG. 03).

3 Attach a beautiful pendant to a lobster clasp with a jump ring (FIG. 04).

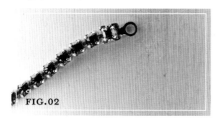
FIG.02

FIG.03

FIG.04

make the necklace

1 String a brass spacer bead, a bead cone, a 6-mm crystal, and a spacer bead onto a 20-gauge balled head pin and finish with a wrapped loop. Repeat on the other side.

2 Cut 12 pieces of leather (three from each color), 15 inches (38.1 cm) long.

3 Glue the ends of the leather into the bead cones. It helps to use a clothespin to hold the pieces of leather together (FIG. 05).

FIG.05

put it all together

1 Slide the rings onto the leather neckpiece.

2 Attach the large lobster-claw clasp to the bead cones with jump rings (FIG. 06).

3 Clip the dangles in between the rings, hooking them to just three strands.

FIG.06

marie antoinette

This is one of those pieces where you can let the beads and ribbon say it all. I love how the wave-shaped plane of the beads is repeated in the undulations of the lovely silk ribbon.

methodology

1 String all the wavy pink beads onto the beading wire, separating each with two gunmetal spacers (FIG. 01).

FIG.01

2 On each end of the wire, string on one gunmetal spacer bead, a crimp bead, and a jump ring. Make a loop in each end by running the wire through the crimp bead, then crimp it to secure it (FIG. 02). Cut off the excess beading wire.

FIG.02

3 Cut the ribbon in half. Tie one end of one piece to one of the jump rings (FIG. 03). Repeat, attaching the remaining piece of ribbon to the other jump ring.

FIG.03

4 Add a drop of fabric adhesive to the top of the knot (FIG. 04) and tie again.

FIG.04

Ribbon wraps and winds around metal beads, adding emphasis to the antique finish. A clip-on bail finding allows you to wear the necklace dressed up with a touch of sparkle, or leave it off for a more casual look.

helios

COLLECT

27 gold round beads, 6 mm

24 round silver beads, 10 mm

Silver filigree and crystal pendant, 50 mm

20 inches (50.8 cm) of 49-strand .015-inch (.38 mm) gold beading wire

1 yard (91.4 cm) of black grosgrain ribbon, ⅜ inch (1 cm) wide

2 round gold crimp findings, 4.5 mm

Two 20-gauge gold jump rings, 5 mm

Silver toggle clasp, 23 mm

Interchangeable crystal bail finding, 16 x 6 mm

INSTRUMENTS

Wire cutters

Small flat-head screwdriver

Large-eye needle

Scissors

Round-nose pliers

TECHNIQUES

Crimping

Opening and closing a jump ring

DIMENSIONS

18.5 inches (47 cm) long

methodology
create the beaded strand

1 Thread one end of the beading wire through a crimp finding, slide on a jump ring, then thread the wire through the crimp finding and close the finding to secure the loop. Thread the opposite end onto a large-eye needle (FIG. 01).

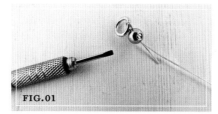

FIG.01

2 Fold one end of the ribbon under and string onto the needle followed by a gold bead (FIG. 02).

FIG.02

3 Wrap the ribbon around to the other side of the gold bead and finish pushing the needle through the bead and the ribbon. Repeat, alternating silver and gold beads (FIG. 03). After the twelfth silver bead, string two gold beads with the ribbon still weaving between each bead—the pendant will sit between these gold beads.

4 Repeat the stringing pattern on the other side until you reach the end of the necklace.

FIG.03

5 Secure one half of the clasp to the end of the wire with a jump ring and a crimp finding (FIG. 04). Attach the other end of the clasp to the jump ring on the other side.

FIG.04

create the pendant

1 Open the loop on the bail and attach the pendant, then close the loop (FIG. 05).

2 Unclasp the bail and clip onto the center of the necklace.

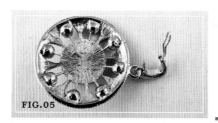

FIG.05

scarlet

This piece is really easy to make, but it's bold and I love it! Bamboo coral comes in many shades, so pick your power color and create a statement.

COLLECT

15 tube-shaped bamboo coral beads, approximately 25 x 10 mm

30 round bamboo coral beads, 7 mm

21 silver spacers, 4 mm

9 shell spacers, 4 mm

9 small silver spacers, 3 mm

27 inches (68.6 cm) of 20-gauge silver wire

20 inches (50.8 cm) of 49-strand .018-inch (.46 mm) nylon-coated beading wire

22 gunmetal crimp beads

Silver hammered hook-and-eye clasp, 18.2 mm

Liver of sulfur solution

Pumice powder

Dish soap

INSTRUMENTS

Wire cutters

Micro butane torch

Chasing hammer

Steel bench block

Round-nose pliers

Brass brush

TECHNIQUES

Using a torch/balling up wire

Hammering

Adding patina

DIMENSIONS

16.5 inches (41.9 cm) long

methodology

create the dangles

1 Cut a piece of silver wire 2¼ inches (5.7 cm) long. Use the torch to create a ball at each end of the wire (FIG. 01). Repeat to make nine balled wires.

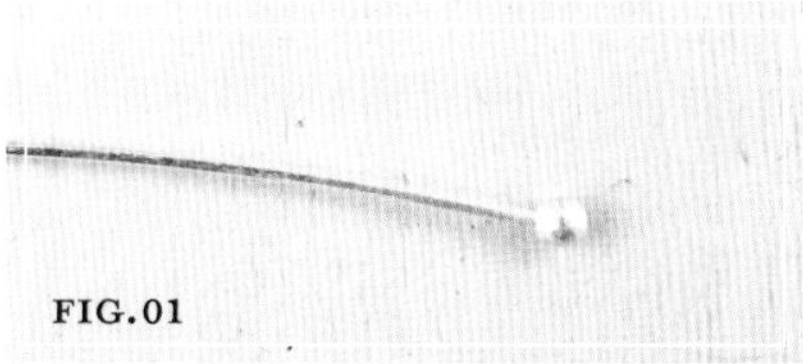

FIG.01

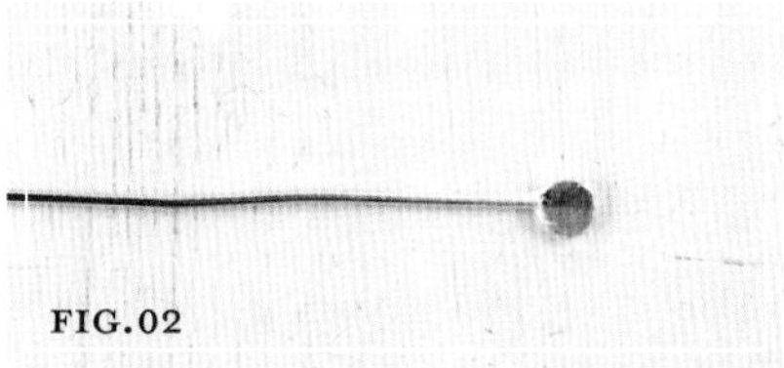

FIG.02

2 Hammer the balled end of the wires with the round face of the chasing hammer on a steel bench block (FIG. 02).

3 String one tube coral bead, a 4-mm silver spacer, a shell spacer, and a small 3-mm silver spacer onto each wire and finish with a wrapped loop. Apply a liver of sulfur patina to each dangle. Pumice the silver wires to remove the patina from the high points and brush with a brass brush and dish soap (FIG. 03).

FIG.03

FIG.04

string the necklace

1 String three round coral beads, a 4-mm silver spacer, a tube coral bead, and a 4-mm silver spacer onto the beading wire. Repeat this sequence two more times followed by two round coral beads.

2 String a coral dangle and a round coral bead onto the wire. Repeat this sequence eight more times (FIG. 04).

3 String the second half of the necklace to mirror the first half.

FIG.05

4 String a row of 11 gunmetal crimp beads onto the beading wire followed by one half of the clasp. Thread the wire end back through the first crimp bead and crimp (FIG. 05). Trim the wire. Repeat on the other side with the other half of the clasp and 11 crimp beads.

NECKLACEOLOGY

67

watch works

Steampunk-style jewelry: I stumbled across an old watchmaker's box of loot at our local antique store—quite the score! Did you know that humans have kept time using methods as varied as water clocks, oil lamp clocks, graduated candles, and calibrated incense sticks?

methodology

Attach the brass chain to the end links on the silver chain. Make adjustments so the two are the same length.

create the charms

First, oxidize anything that's made of copper or silver with liver of sulfur to antique the components. Scuff the washers and watch faces with coarse sandpaper to give them a scratchy texture (FIG. 01). (Practice on a scrap metal surface first to see if you like the effect.)

FIG. 01

charm #1

1 This will hang at the center of the necklace. String one tiny washer, a hammered brass daisy spacer (I hammered this one flat on

FIG. 02

FIG. 03

a steel bench block), a large hammered washer, a watch face, a large wheel, a watch face, and a brass washer onto a bolt (FIG. 02). Screw the nut so everything is snug and cut the end so that 1 mm remains. Lay the piece on a bench block and hammer flat to create a rivet head (FIG. 03).

2 String one brass spacer, a 6-mm silver bead, and a brass spacer onto a head pin and finish with a wrapped loop. Repeat to make two more bead dangles. Connect one dangle to the 10-mm brass jump ring. Set the other two

aside to use in Charm #5.

3 If desired, apply alcohol ink to the clock hands charm. Attach the clock hands charm, the 10-mm brass jump ring, and a washer to a loop on the wheel. Hang on the center link of the chain with a square jump ring (FIG. 04).

FIG. 04

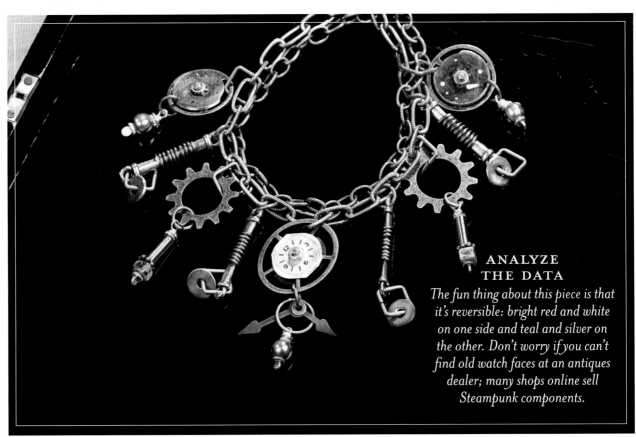

ANALYZE THE DATA

The fun thing about this piece is that it's reversible: bright red and white on one side and teal and silver on the other. Don't worry if you can't find old watch faces at an antiques dealer; many shops online sell Steampunk components.

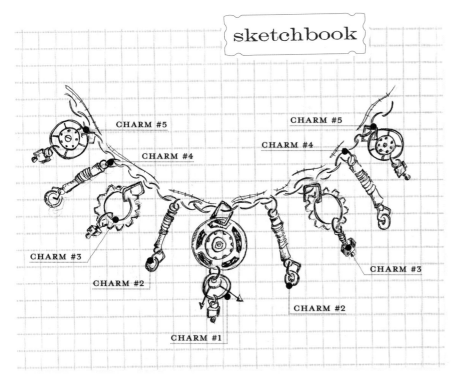

CHARM #5

CHARM #4

CHARM #5

CHARM #4

CHARM #3

CHARM #2

CHARM #3

CHARM #2

CHARM #1

bolt. Finish the bolt as you did for the center charm. Repeat to make a second charm.

3 Hang another silver bead dangle like the one in the center charm at the bottom of the gear. Skip one silver link/two brass links and connect to the necklace with a square jump ring. Repeat to make a pair.

FIG. 06

4 Finish the ends of the chain by connecting the lock end of the toggle to the necklace with a 6-mm silver jump ring and the key with the 5-mm jump ring (FIG. 06).

charms #2 and #4

1 Coil ½ inch (1.3 cm) of brass wire around the center of a bar link (FIG. 05). Attach a washer to a square jump ring and hang on one of the bar link loops. Skip one silver link/two brass links and connect the charm to the necklace with a small brass jump ring. Repeat to make three more.

2 Skip one silver link/two brass links and connect another bar link charm to the necklace with a small brass jump ring.

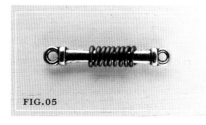

FIG.05

charm #3

1 String one brass spacer, a cube bead, a daisy spacer, a coiled bead, and a brass spacer onto a head pin and finish with a wrapped loop. Connect this dangle to a gear. Hammer a copper jump ring flat on the steel block. Skip one silver link/ two brass links and connect the gear and ring to the necklace with a square jump ring. Repeat to make a second charm.

charm #5

1 If desired, color the back of the watch face with alcohol ink, then scratch with sandpaper to create texture.

2 String a tiny silver washer, a watch face, a gear charm, and a hammered silver washer onto a

COLLECT

28 black pearls, 8 mm

28 gray oval bead separators, 1.5 mm

9 faceted shell beads, 8 mm

3 double-drilled shell donut beads, 20 mm

7 silver daisy spacer beads, 6 mm

7 plum purple fire-polished rondelle beads, 5 x 2 mm

3 dark purple rondelle beads, 5 mm

4 purple fire-polished round beads, 5 mm

20 inches (50.8 cm) of 49-strand .018-inch (.46 mm) beading wire

5 inches (12.7 cm) of gray polyester chain, 8 mm

Silver duet clasp, 31.75 mm

Two 20-gauge gunmetal jump rings, 5 mm

9 gunmetal jump rings, 8 mm

Silver twisted ring, 16 mm

2 silver twisted rings, 10 mm

4 silver hammered rings, 27 mm

8 diamond-cut silver rings, 20 mm

2 silver rings, 12 mm

4 silver crimp findings, 3.5 mm

7 silver balled head pins

Liver of sulfur solution

Dish soap

INSTRUMENTS

Brass brush

Small screwdriver

Round-nose pliers

Chain-nose pliers

TECHNIQUES

Adding patina

Crimping

Wrapped loop

Opening and closing a jump ring

DIMENSIONS

17 inches (43.2 cm)

orion

It's in the stars: This necklace is a fashion must-have. Round and round we go, layering circles within circles from a strand of pearl baubles.

methodology
create the necklace

1 Dip all of the silver findings into liver of sulfur to make them a gunmetal finish. Brush each with a brass brush and dish soap.

2 Attach a 5-mm jump ring to each end of the duet clasp. Secure the beading wire to the jump ring with a crimp finding (FIG. 01).

FIG.01

ends to the clasp with a crimp finding.

embellish the necklace

1 String one donut shell bead with a faceted bead in the center, a spacer bead, a plum purple rondelle, and a dark purple rondelle onto a head pin and finish with a wrapped loop. Repeat to make two more dangles (FIG. 04).

FIG.04

2 String a faceted shell bead, a silver spacer bead, a plum purple rondelle, and a 5-mm purple bead onto a head pin and finish with a wrapped loop. Repeat to make three more dangles.

3 Starting at the center of the polyester chain, attach the large twisted ring and a donut shell dangle with an 8-mm jump ring.

4 Moving outward, skip one link and attach a small twisted ring, a large hammered ring, and a shell bead dangle with an 8-mm jump ring. Repeat for the opposite side.

5 Skip one link and attach a donut dangle and a 20-mm silver ring with an 8-mm jump ring. Repeat for the opposite side.

3 String a pearl and a bead separator onto the beading wire. Repeat 12 more times, followed by a faceted shell bead, a bead separator, and a pearl. Repeat to create a second strand (FIG. 02).

FIG.02

FIG.03

4 Attach the ends of wire nearest the shell beads to the polyester chain with a crimp finding (FIG. 03). Attach the opposite

FIG.05

7 Skip one link and attach a 20-mm ring and a 12-mm ring with an 8-mm jump ring. Repeat for the opposite side (FIG. 05).

6 Skip one link and attach a 20-mm silver ring, a large hammered ring, and a shell dangle with an 8-mm jump ring. Repeat for the opposite side.

ANALYZE THE DATA

Lots of textures keep things interesting. I like mixing faceted beads, twisted wire, hammered rings, thread–wrapped chain, pearly finishes, and high polish.

tranquility

I designed this piece after sailing from San Diego to Catalina Island. The magic of seeing dolphins jumping alongside the boat was breathtaking. I'll never forget that feeling of calm out on the water.

COLLECT

Copper seed beads,
  2 grams
Navy seed beads,
  2 grams
10 copper daisy spacers,
  5 mm
4 copper bicone-
  shaped beads, 15 mm
6 blue faceted Czech
  beads, 9 x 6 mm
6 copper spacers, 4 mm
2 shell beads, 16 mm
86 multicolored droplet
  beads, 8 x 5 mm
45 inches (1.1 m) of
  19-strand .015-inch
  (.38 mm) copper
  beading wire
2 copper crimp findings
Bronze shell clasp,
  17 mm

INSTRUMENTS

Wire cutters
Small screwdriver

TECHNIQUES

Crimping

DIMENSIONS

18.5 inches (47 cm) long

ANALYZE THE DATA

So many clasps are ho-hum. Keep your eyes peeled for really interesting ones and snag them. Don't worry if you can't use them now. They're worth keeping around until the perfect necklace-making opportunity comes around.

methodology

1 Cut two pieces of beading wire 20 inches (50.8 cm) long.

2 String 3 inches (7.6 cm) of copper and navy seed beads in no particular order onto each piece of beading wire (FIG. 01).

FIG.01

3 Next, string a copper daisy spacer, a bicone bead, a copper daisy spacer, a blue Czech bead, a 4-mm copper spacer, a shell bead, a 4-mm copper spacer, a blue Czech bead, a daisy spacer, a copper bicone-shaped bead, and a daisy spacer onto both wires, holding the wires together as one strand (FIG. 02).

FIG.02

4 String a row of 43 droplet beads onto *each* beading wire, so that you now have two strands (FIG. 03).

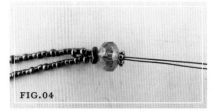

FIG.03

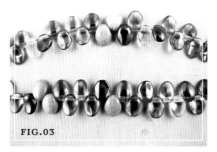

FIG.04

5 String the other half of the necklace so it mirrors the first half (FIG. 04).

6 String a 4-mm copper spacer, a blue Czech bead, and a daisy spacer over both wires held together as one strand on each end of the necklace. Finish the ends with a crimp finding, connecting each side to the shell clasp (FIG. 05).

FIG.05

COLLECT

3 oval shell links,
   35 x 25 mm

4 oval metal links,
   17 x 30 mm

16 purple faceted fire-
   polished Czech glass
   beads, 5 mm

18 brass daisy spacer
   beads, 5 mm

9 yellow and copper
   round faceted beads,
   6 mm

16 round ridge-cut
   copper spacer beads,
   5 mm

8 purple pressed-glass
   Czech beads, 14 mm

2 grams of brushed
   copper tube beads,
   4 mm

1½ yards (1.4 m) of
   hand-dyed silk rib-
   bon in Terrazzo, ⁷⁄₁₆
   inch (1.1 cm) wide

40 inches (1 m) of
   7-strand .018-inch
   (.46 mm) satin cop-
   per beading wire

2 brass crimp beads

Brass flower clasp,
   22 mm

Thick white glue

INSTRUMENTS

Crimping pliers

TECHNIQUES

Crimping

DIMENSIONS

18.5 inches (47 cm)

plum tree

You could wrap anything with delicate hand-dyed silk ribbon and it would look beautiful. Here, metal and shell elements are wrapped to create covered links with beads woven in and out.

methodology
wrap the links

1 Everyone wraps differently, so use a scrap piece of ribbon to determine the length you will need for each link.

2 Secure one end of the ribbon to a link with thick white glue and leave to dry (FIG. 01). Wrap the tail of ribbon around the link so it just slightly overlaps, and secure

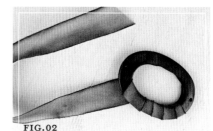

FIG.02

the end with a drop of glue. Repeat for all seven links (FIG. 02).

string the necklace

1 Cut two pieces of beading wire 22 inches (55.9 cm) long. Onto both wires held together, string one crimp bead, a purple fire-polished bead, a daisy spacer, a yellow and copper round faceted bead, a copper ridge-cut bead, a daisy spacer, a

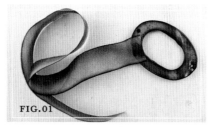

FIG.01

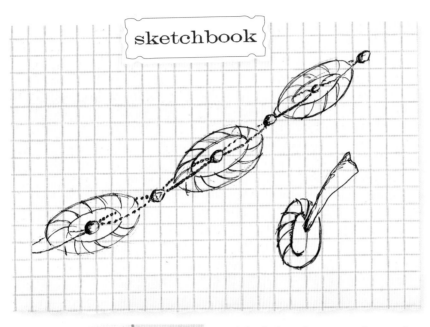

sketchbook

4 String three copper tube beads onto each wire, separating them, and position a large shell link so one wire is on top and one is underneath. String a copper tube bead, a purple fire-polished bead, a yellow and copper round faceted bead, a purple fire-polished bead, and a copper tube bead onto both wires. Position the wires so one is on top and one is underneath the shell link (FIG. 06).

FIG.06

14-mm Czech bead, a daisy spacer, and a ridge-cut bead (FIG. 03).

2 String three copper tube beads onto *each* wire, so you're now working with two strands instead of one, and position a small shell link so one wire is on top and one is underneath. Holding the wires together once again, string on a purple fire-polished bead, a yellow and copper round faceted bead, and a purple fire-polished bead; this locks the link in place. Separate the wires again and string three more copper tube beads onto each, then position the wires so one is lying on top

FIG.03

of the link and one is underneath (FIG. 04).

FIG.04

3 String one copper bead, a daisy spacer, a 14-mm Czech bead, a daisy spacer, and a copper bead onto both wires (FIG. 05).

FIG.05

5 Repeat, alternating small ribbon links, 14-mm Czech beads, and large ribbon links until you reach the last small ribbon link and row of beads.

6 Thread the ends of the wire through the loops on the clasp, then back through the crimp beads; crimp (FIG. 07).

FIG.07

art nouveau

One look at this brass pendant and you can immediately see the sinuous lines and floral elements from one of my favorite periods in design: art nouveau.

COLLECT

22 cathedral-cut black and
gold Czech beads, 6 mm
40 brass twist bead caps,
8 mm
20 round faceted jasper
beads, 9 mm
Brass focal pendant,
90 x 50 mm
20 black Czech faceted
beads, 4 mm
20 fire-polished multicolor
beads in black and cop-
per, 5 x 3 mm
20 fire-polished copper and
clear Czech beads, 4 mm
22 round copper beads,
4 mm
Silver spacer bead, 6 mm
40 inches (1 m) of
copper beading wire
17½ inches (44.5 cm) of
large brass chain
15 inches (38.1 cm) of
small brass chain
2 four-loop end bars,
30 x 5 mm
8 brass crimp beads
22 brass jump rings, 6 mm
Toggle clasp finding,
27 x 6 mm
Gunmetal balled head pin
Brass hook, 25 x 10 mm

INSTRUMENTS

Wire cutters
Crimping pliers
Chain-nose pliers
Round-nose pliers
Awl
Wooden block
with a hole

TECHNIQUES

Crimping
Opening and closing
a jump ring
Wrapped loop

DIMENSIONS

20 inches (50.8 cm)

sketchbook

methodology

1 String a black and gold cathedral-cut bead, a bead cap, a large
jasper bead, and a bead cap onto the
beading wire. Continue this pattern
until you have strung a total of 10
jasper beads (FIG. 01). String one
cathedral-cut bead. Place the end
bars side by side in front of you with

FIG.01

the loops at the bottom. Secure one
end of the beading wire to the bar

on the right, third loop in from the left, with a crimp bead. Secure the opposite end to a jump ring with a crimp bead. Repeat for the second bar except connect the beading wire to the third loop in from the right.

2 String an assortment of the remaining beads onto the beading wire in a random pattern (FIG. 02). Secure one end of the beading wire to the

FIG.02

first loop on the right bar with a crimp bead. Connect the opposite end to a jump ring with a crimp bead. Repeat for the second bar. Optionally, you can add crimp bead covers to the crimped sections. Here I made my own with the small copper beads with a seam. Slide the bead onto an awl and poke down into a block with a hole in it to pry the bead open (FIG. 03). Close as you would a normal crimp bead.

FIG.03

3 Cut the large chain into two pieces measuring 8¾ inches (22.2 cm) long. Connect it to the outer loops on the end bar.

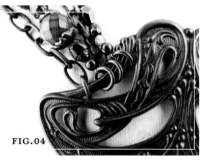

FIG.04

4 Cut the small chain into two pieces 7½ inches (19 cm) long. Connect it to the remaining loops on the end bar.

5 Using FIG. 04 as a guide, attach each of the pieces to the brass pendant with jump rings.

FIG.05

6 Attach a jump ring in between each of the strands to create space (FIG. 05).

7 String the silver spacer bead onto the balled head pin followed by the toggle end of the clasp. Make a bend ⅜ inch (1 mm) from

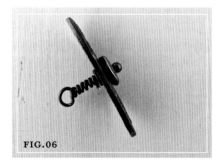

FIG.06

the back of the toggle and finish with a wrapped loop (FIG. 06).

8 Attach the clasp and the hook to the single loop on the end bar (FIG. 07).

FIG.07

vanuatu

COLLECT

Silver round bezel-frame pendant, 30 mm

Vintage glass handpainted cabachon, 28 x 15 mm

25 to 30 small pebbles, 3 mm

4 brown rondelle beads, 5 mm

8 brass spacer beads, 4 mm

6 bronze glass faceted beads, 4 x 2 mm

2 quartz beads, 8 mm

2 gray and brown cube beads, 4 mm

2 silver spacer beads, 4 x 2 mm

Fish charm, 12 x 14 mm

2-inch (5.1 cm) piece of gunmetal chain, 7.6 mm

Four 25-inch (63.5 cm) strands of silk cord in light brown, dark brown, yellow, and multicolor

Two 18-gauge silver jump rings, 6 mm

Three 18-gauge brass jump rings, 6 mm

7 silver jump rings, 5 mm

2 twisted silver rings, 23 mm

6 silver balled head pins

2 silver fold-over end crimps with loops, 12 x 5 mm

Silver lobster clasp, 10 mm

Epoxy clay

Brown acrylic paint

Liver of sulfur solution (optional)

INSTRUMENTS

Paintbrush

Soft cloth

Steel bench block

Chasing hammer

Large-eye needle

Round-nose pliers

Chain-nose pliers

Scissors

TECHNIQUES

Epoxy resin clay

Hammering

Adding patina

Wrapped loop

Opening and closing a jump ring

DIMENSIONS

20.5 inches (52.1 cm)

Have you ever made your own stepping stone with broken glass? It's as simple as pushing the pieces into clay. The process here is much the same, so you can incorporate tiny treasures into your pendant.

methodology

make the pendant

Fill the bezel with epoxy clay. Press the cabochon into the middle and press tiny pebbles around the outside. Once the epoxy clay sets up, stain with brown paint. I like to mix a drop of paint with a teaspoon of water and brush it on. Afterward, wipe away the top of the cabochon and pebbles with a soft cloth (FIG. 01).

assemble the necklace

1 Attach two 18-gauge silver jump rings to the pendant and an 18-gauge brass jump ring in the middle of the silver rings.

FIG.01

2 Thread three of the four cords through the rings and make an overhand knot to secure the pendant in the middle of the cords (FIG. 02).

FIG.02

3 Hammer the twisted rings flat on the steel bench block. You can also apply a liver of sulfur patina to the rings to antique them.

4 String a twisted ring on either side of the pendant and knot in place.

5 Make two more knots on both sides approximately 1 inch (2.5 cm) apart (FIG. 03).

FIG.03

6 Thread a large-eye needle with the fourth silk strand and run through all the knots. This adds a different line of interest to the strands and cuts down on the bulkiness of the knots (FIG. 04).

FIG.04

7 String one brown bead, a brass spacer, and a bronze bead onto a head pin and finish with a wrapped loop. Repeat to make three more dangles.

FIG.05

8 String one brass spacer, a quartz bead, a brass spacer, a cube bead, a silver spacer, and a bronze bead onto a head pin and finish with a wrapped loop (FIG. 05). Repeat to make a second dangle.

FIG.06

FIG.07

9 Connect two small beaded dangles to each twisted ring with 5-mm silver jump rings and the quartz dangle in the middle with a 6-mm brass jump ring (FIG. 06).

10 Cut the silk strands to the desired length and finish the ends with the fold-over loop findings (FIG. 07).

11 Attach the clasp and chain to the end loops with a 5-mm jump ring. Hang the fish charm on the end of the chain with a 5-mm jump ring (FIG. 08).

FIG.08

odalisque

These opulent golden rings and brilliant jewel tones make me think of the Ottoman empire.

COLLECT

15 green glass rondelles,
    4 x 3 mm
18 brass daisy spacers, 5 mm
7 aqua teardrop glass beads,
    23 x 18 mm
4 gold glass rondelles,
    8 x 5 mm
Green seed beads, 2 grams
Square shell focal pendant,
    55 mm
3 purple bicone beads,
    6 mm
15 inches (38.1 cm) of
    elongated brass chain,
    5 x 3 mm
16 inches (40.6 cm) of
    49-strand .015-inch
    (.38 mm) gold beading
    wire
10 inches (25.4 cm) of
    20-gauge brass wire
2 gold crimp findings
2 brass wire guards, 4.57 mm
2 hammered brass rings,
    34 mm
2 hammered brass rings,
    24 mm
12 brass jump rings, 10 mm
3 brass jump rings, 6 mm
Brass jump ring, 5 mm
Hammered brass toggle
    clasp, 18 mm

INSTRUMENTS

Wire cutters
Crimping pliers
Round-nose pliers

TECHNIQUES

Crimping
Opening and closing
    a jump ring
Wrapped loop

DIMENSIONS

24 inches (61 cm)

methodology

Start by cutting two pieces of chain, each 3 inches (7.6 cm) long. Set them aside for the time being.

left side

1 String one green rondelle, a daisy spacer, a teardrop bead (pointed end first), a daisy spacer, a green rondelle, a gold rondelle, a green rondelle, and a daisy spacer onto the beading wire. Repeat the sequence once more.

2 String one teardrop bead (pointed end first), a daisy spacer, a green rondelle, and a crimp finding onto the strand.

3 String on the end links on the two pieces of chain and 20 seed beads, and thread the tail of wire through the center of the shell pendant and back through the crimp finding, leaving you with a beaded loop (FIG. 01).

FIG.01

4 Thread the opposite end of the wire through the crimp finding and a wire guard. Crimp.

right side

1 String one green rondelle, a daisy spacer, a teardrop bead (pointed end first), a daisy spacer, a green rondelle, a gold rondelle, a green rondelle, a daisy spacer, a purple bicone, a daisy spacer, a purple bicone, a daisy spacer, a purple bicone, a daisy spacer, a green rondelle, a gold rondelle, a daisy spacer, a teardrop bead (round end first), a daisy spacer, and a green rondelle onto the beading wire.

2 Finish the ends as you did for the other side.

3 Cut 12 pieces of chain 1¼ inches (3.2 cm) long.

4 Attach three sections of chain to the wire guard attached to the beaded strand (FIG. 02). Thread the wire back through the crimp finding, then crimp the finding. Attach the opposite ends of the chain to one large and one small hammered brass ring with three 10-mm jump rings.

FIG.02

5 Attach three more sections of chain to the opposite side of the hammered rings with three 10-mm jump rings (FIG. 03). Repeat for the opposite side of the necklace.

FIG.03

6 String a green rondelle, a
daisy spacer, a teardrop bead,
a daisy spacer, and a green rondelle
onto the brass wire. Finish each end
with a wrapped loop (FIG. 04). Repeat to make one more beaded link.

FIG.04

FIG.05

7 Attach the end pieces of chain
to the beaded link with a
6-mm jump ring so the round end
of the teardrop is closest to the
chain. Attach the opposite end of
the beaded link to the loop end of
the clasp with a 6-mm jump ring.
Repeat for the opposite side for the
chain pieces (FIG. 05). Attach the
toggle end of the clasp with a 5-mm
jump ring.

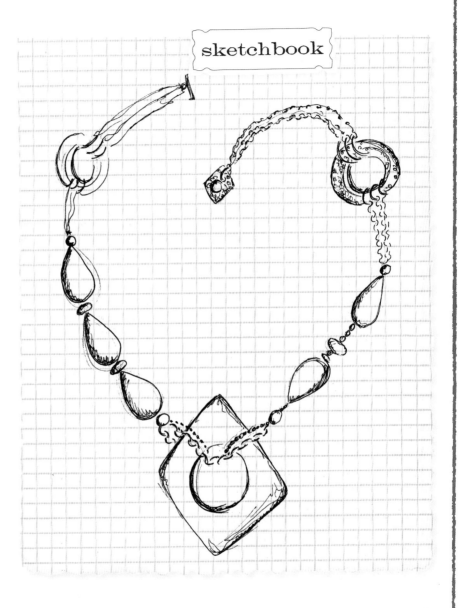

sketchbook

argus

It would be impossible to re-create this piece exactly. So many of the elements will be found in flea markets or your grandma's button box, and that's what makes it so interesting. I'll show you the basics, and you can then let your imagination go to town.

COLLECT

Vintage clip-on earrings
Large and small filigree
   pieces
Focal cabochon in
   setting (this was a
   pendant)
Peacock feather
Velvet leaves
Glass buttons
Ribbon necklace find-
   ing, 18 inches
   (45.7 cm) long
Decorative clasp
Piece of soft fabric or
   felt (optional)
220-grit sandpaper
Jeweler's adhesive

INSTRUMENTS

Heavy-duty wire
   cutters
Scissors
Round-nose pliers
Chain-nose pliers

TECHNIQUES

Opening and closing
   a jump ring

DIMENSIONS

22 inches (55.9 cm) long

EXPERIMENT

*Choose a focal piece or
color theme and build
around that. Find large,
flat filigree pieces that
can be glued to, or easily
linked with, jump rings.
Clip–on earrings and
glass buttons make the
best filler.*

methodology

NOTE: *When shooting FIGS. 01 to 06, I had to use other elements than the ones shown on page 90.*

1 Cut away any loops or earring findings with heavy-duty wire cutters (FIG. 01). Sand jagged edges with sandpaper if needed.

FIG.01

2 Lay your filigree pieces out, creating a slight curve; this will form the bib of the necklace (FIG. 02). Be sure to position the outside pieces so there are holes or loops to connect the clasp and ribbon to. Glue together at the joins.

FIG.02

3 Put your focal piece in place. Add a feather or velvet leaves under the focal piece and attach with adhesive (FIG. 03).

FIG.03

FIG.04

4 Embellish outward from the focal piece with velvet flowers with earring findings on top, and buttons and small pieces around the bottom (FIG. 04).

FIG.05

5 Attach one end of the ribbon necklace to a loop on a filigree piece. Attach the clasp to the opposite end of the necklace and filigree piece (FIG. 05).

6 Optionally, you can cut a piece of soft fabric or felt and adhere it to the back if you want to hide all the connections (FIG. 06).

FIG.06

pod

Like seeds clustered inside of fruit, these little green beads are equally rife with possibility!

COLLECT

4 lime jade beads, 2 mm

11 brass beads with ridges, 4 mm

10 grossular garnet faceted tabiz briolettes, 10 x 10 mm

8 inches (20.3 cm) of cable chain, 3 mm

20 inches (50.8 cm) of brass chain, 5 mm

6 inches (15.2 cm) of 49-strand .018-inch (.46 mm) beading wire

11 brass balled head pins

5 brass jump rings, 5 mm

18-gauge brass jump ring, 6 mm

Twisted silver jump ring, 5 mm

2 brass crimp beads

Brass lobster clasp, 7 mm

INSTRUMENTS

Heavy-duty wire cutters

Round-nose pliers

Crimping pliers

TECHNIQUES

Crimping

Opening and closing a jump ring

Wrapped loop

DIMENSIONS

Chain, 21 inches (53.3 cm) long; tassel, 4 inches (10.2 cm) long

EXPERIMENT

There are so many gorgeous gemstones available—just because I used jade doesn't mean you have to. Change it up!

methodology

1 Cut four pieces of cable chain 1¾ inches (4.4 cm) long.

2 String a 2-mm lime jade bead and a ridged brass bead onto a balled head pin, begin making a wrapped loop, attach it to the end of a chain piece, and close the loop (FIG. 01). Repeat to attach a lime jade bead dangle to each end of a chain.

FIG.01

3 Secure a piece of beading wire to the jump ring connected to the chain tassel with a brass crimp bead (FIG. 02).

4 String three briolettes, one bead dangle, a briolette, and a bead dangle onto the beading wire and continue alternating briolettes and bead dangles to the end, finishing with a briolette (FIG. 03).

FIG.02

FIG.03

5 Secure the end of the beading wire to the 18-gauge jump ring with a crimp bead.

6 Cut the brass chain in half. Connect the ends of the brass chain to the twisted jump ring and the 18-gauge jump ring with 5-mm jump rings (FIG. 04).

FIG.04

7 Connect each part of the lobster clasp to the ends of the brass chain with 5-mm jump rings (FIG. 05).

FIG.05

COLLECT

2 oval end cones,
   14 x 20 mm
2 copper bead caps,
   10 mm
2 silver spacers,
   1 x 5 mm
2 silver spacers,
   1 x 4 mm
2 fire-polished plum
   Czech beads, 5 mm
10 inches (25.4 cm) of
   7-strand .015-inch
   (.38 mm) red beading
   wire
Two 18-gauge silver
   jump rings, 6 mm
4 crimp beads
Base metal S hook,
   23 x 5 mm
1 skein of novelty yarn

INSTRUMENTS

Size G (4 mm)
   crochet hook
Quilter's ruler
Scissors
Wire cutters
Crimping pliers

TECHNIQUES

Crochet
Crimping
Opening and closing
   a jump ring

DIMENSIONS

24 inches (61 cm) long

ANALYZE THE DATA

I love how the copper bead caps pick up the rust color in my ribbon yarn! I brought the yarn with me to the bead shop so I could choose beads that would bring out the purple tones in the fiber.

harvest moon

The harvest moon is breathtaking with its intense orange colors against the fall sky. The colors in the novelty yarn I used remind me of those stunning nights when the glow of the moon illuminates a layer of frost on ripe pumpkins.

methodology

1 Using the novelty yarn and the crochet hook, chain 21 strands, each measuring from 18 to 20 inches (45.7 to 50.8 cm) long (FIG. 01). Leave a 2-inch (5.1 cm) tail on both ends of each strand. A quilter's ruler comes in handy here so you can lay out your strands as you crochet to make them graduated in size.

FIG.01

2 Hold your piece up to check the drape of the strands and fill in or adjust if needed.

sketchbook

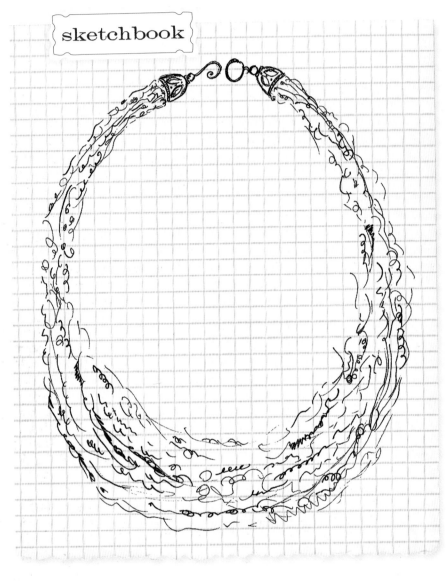

and string a crimp bead over both ends of the wire. Crimp (FIG. 03).

5 String a large end cone, a copper bead cap, a large silver spacer, a plum bead, a small silver spacer, and a crimp bead onto each wire (FIG. 04).

FIG.04

6 Thread the wire through the jump ring and back through the crimp bead. Remove the slack and crimp. Trim the excess wire. Repeat for the opposite side.

7 Attach the S hook to the jump rings (FIG. 05).

FIG.05

3 Group the ends together and make a knot (FIG. 02).

FIG.02

FIG.03

4 Cut two 5-inch (12.7 cm) pieces of beading wire. Thread the wire through the knot

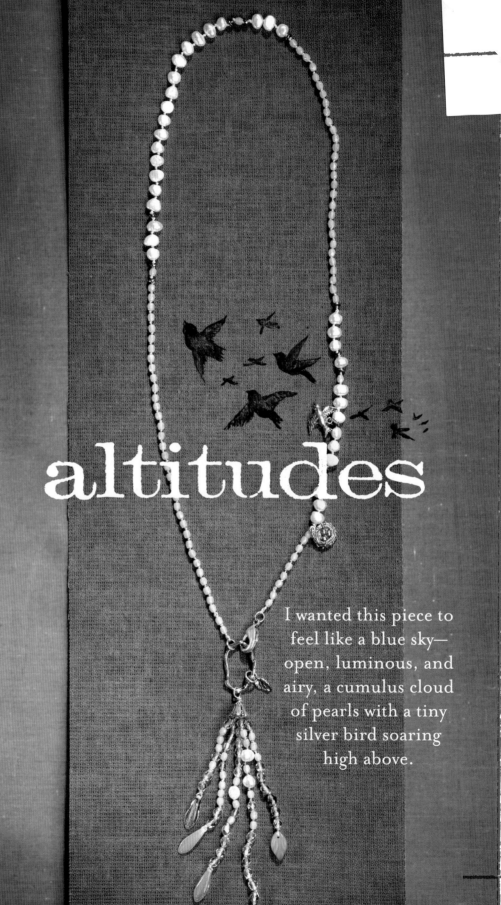

COLLECT

98 blue Czech glass beads, 3 mm

10 silver spacer beads, 5 mm

37 white freshwater pearls, 6 mm

15 aqua fire-polished Czech faceted beads, 6 mm

14 clear faceted Czech beads, 4 mm

3 blue teardrop beads, 15 x 5 mm

2 blue Czech leaf beads, 13 x 5 mm

2 silver bird-themed charms (nest and bird), approximately 12 mm

Silver leaf charm, 7 mm

Silver bead cone, 10 x 5 mm

6 yards (5.4 m) of cream-colored silk or nylon cord

5 inches (12.7 cm) of 20-gauge silver wire

4 silver jump rings, 15 mm

Silver twig ring, 14 x 25 mm

Silver lobster clasp, 15 mm

INSTRUMENTS

Collapsible beading needle

Knotting tool

Chain-nose pliers

Round-nose pliers

Wire cutters

TECHNIQUES

Knotting

Opening and closing a jump ring

Wrapped loop

DIMENSIONS

24 inches (61 cm) long

altitudes

I wanted this piece to feel like a blue sky— open, luminous, and airy, a cumulus cloud of pearls with a tiny silver bird soaring high above.

methodology
knot the necklace

1 Thread a collapsible needle with silk cord. String 36 blue beads, a silver spacer, a blue bead, a silver spacer, three pearls, a silver spacer, a blue bead, a silver spacer, 15 pearls, a silver spacer, a blue bead, a silver spacer, three pearls, 32 blue beads, a silver spacer, four pearls, a silver spacer, a blue bead, six pearls, a blue bead, a silver spacer, three pearls, a silver spacer, and nine blue beads onto the cord.

2 Tie one end of the cord to a jump ring and attach the jump ring to the twig ring. (Follow the instructions for knotting on page 20.) Thread the tail of the cord through the first bead and knot the two ends together. Trim the short tail. Use the knotting tool to place knots in between each bead for the entire strand.

3 Knot the opposite end to the lobster clasp (FIG. 01). The lobster clasp will connect to the twig ring as the closure.

FIG.01

create the tassel

1 String the remaining 16 blue beads, the aqua beads, the clear beads, and the remaining three pearls randomly onto a length of silk cord.

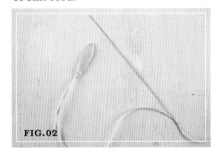

FIG.02

2 The teardrop and leaf beads will be used as the ends of the tassel piece. Tie the end of the cord to a teardrop (FIG. 02) or a leaf bead and begin knotting as you did before. Knot a 2- to 3-inch (5.1 to 7.6 cm) section of beads that you strung in step 1. After the final knot, trim the end, leaving a 3-inch (7.6 cm) tail. Repeat four more times for a total of five tassel pieces (FIG. 03).

FIG.03

3 Make a wrapped loop at one end of the wire. Group the five tassel pieces together, thread the end tails through the wrapped loop, and knot.

4 String the bead cone onto the wire to hide the knot and attach to the twig ring with a wrapped loop. Trim the extra wire (FIG. 04).

FIG.04

5 Attach the bird and nest charms to the long strand with

FIG.05

jump rings, between the fifth and seventh pearls, on the side of the necklace closest to the lobster clasp (FIG. 05).

6 Attach the leaf charm to the twig ring with the final jump ring (FIG. 06).

FIG.06

bittersweet

I like to take the back roads when I drive.
Sometimes I spot vines of bittersweet growing
along rusted wire fences. The plants start out green,
then ripen to a pretty orange and gold. It's a true
sign of autumn here in the American Midwest.

COLLECT

Completely random assortment of approximately 200 beads

Spool of nylon cord in desired color

8 silver-plated bead tips, 3 mm

4 silver-plated 20-gauge jump rings, 5 mm

Two-strand sterling silver box clasp finding, 15 x 12 mm

Adhesive (optional)

INSTRUMENTS

Collapsible beading needle

Size F (5) crochet hook

Tape measure

Scissors

Chain-nose pliers

TECHNIQUES

Bead crochet

Opening and closing a jump ring

DIMENSIONS

20 inches (50.8 cm) long

EXPERIMENT

When wearing the necklace, you can twist the strands together before clasping it, or wear them loosely.

methodology

1 You'll work with the spool of cord, rather than cutting a piece of it. Thread it with the collapsible beading needle, and string on approximately 200 beads (FIG. 01).

FIG.01

2 Secure the tail of cord to the crochet hook with a slipknot (FIG. 02), then chain 3 (FIG. 03).

FIG.02

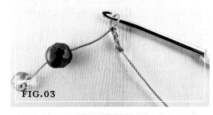

FIG.03

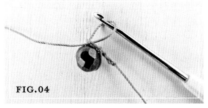

FIG.04

3 Slide a bead up next to the crochet hook and make a chain stitch, locking the bead in place (FIG. 04). Make another chain stitch without a bead and then one with a bead. Continue in this manner (in other words, each bead will be sepa-

rated by a chain stitch) until you've made a strand 18 inches (45.7 cm) long. Cut the cord, leaving 1 inch (2.5 cm), and pull the tail through the last chain to secure it.

FIG.05

FIG.06

4 Repeat steps 1 through 3 to make three more strands that measure 18 inches (45.7 cm).

5 Make a knot at the end of each strand (FIG. 05). Fold over a bead tip on both ends of each strand. If desired, you can apply a dot of adhesive—I always do. Using chain-nose pliers, fold the finding over the knot (FIG. 06).

6 Using a jump ring, attach one end of two of the strands to one loop of the clasp. Attach the other ends of these strands to the corresponding loop on the other half of the clasp. Repeat for the remaining ends (FIG. 07).

FIG.07

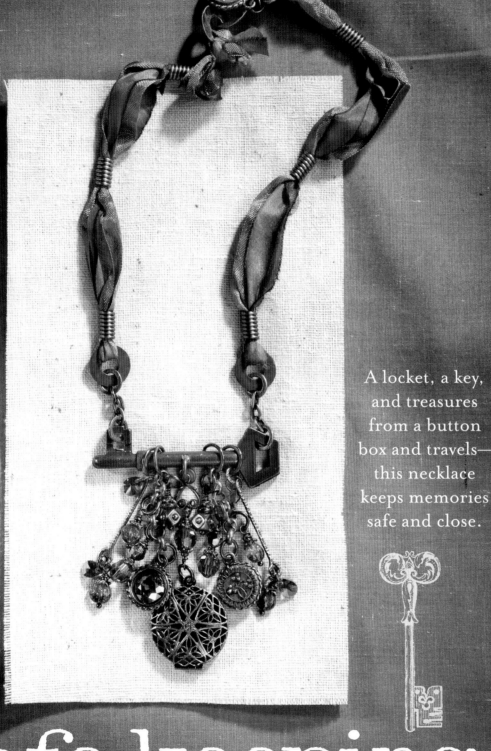

A locket, a key, and treasures from a button box and travels— this necklace keeps memories safe and close.

safe keeping

COLLECT

3 copper washers, 16 mm
Base metal key, 65 mm
2 vintage buttons with shank, 12 mm
Faceted Swarovski rivoli crystal, 8 mm
3 round gunmetal rivoli setting charms, 15 mm
10 gunmetal bead caps, 5 mm
3 Indian Sapphire Swarovski crystals, 8 mm
Gunmetal vine heart link, 13 x 9.5 mm
Silver filigree locket, 28 mm
Brass spacer bead, 6 mm
4 purple and gold glass beads, 6 x 2 mm
2 Silver Night Swarovski crystals, 6 mm
2 gunmetal octagon beads, 5 mm
2 brown glass spacer beads, 5 mm
4 blue Swarovski crystal drops, 6 x 4 mm
6 inches (15 cm) of 18-gauge silver wire
8 inches (20.3 cm) of silver-plated chain, 6.5 mm
1 yard (91.4 cm) of hand-dyed blue ribbon
1 yard (91.4 cm) of hand-dyed gold ribbon
5 copper jump rings, 10 mm
Nine 18-gauge gunmetal jump rings, 6 mm
4 gunmetal jump rings, 5 mm
2 gunmetal jump rings, 3 mm
8 gunmetal balled head pins
4 copper links, 9 mm
Copper hook clasp, 12 x 21 mm
220-, 320-, and 400-grit sandpaper
Liver of sulfur solution
Pumice powder
Dish soap
Multipurpose adhesive
Fabric adhesive

INSTRUMENTS

Steel bench block
Chasing hammer
Brass brush
Center punch
Mallet
Dremel tool and drill bit, ¹⁄₁₆ inch and ³⁄₁₆ inch (1.5 and 4.5 mm)
Heavy-duty wire cutters
Mandrel, 3.4 mm
Wire cutters
Chain-nose pliers
Round-nose pliers

TECHNIQUES

Hammering
Adding patina
Drilling
Coiling
Opening and closing a jump ring
Wrapped loop

DIMENSIONS

20 inches (50.8 cm)

methodology
prepare the elements

Washer Links

Sand the copper washers lightly with all three grits listed, starting with the 220 grit and moving on to

FIG. 01

400. Lay the washers on a steel bench block and hammer one side with the round face of the chasing hammer (FIG. 01). Apply a liver of sulfur patina to the washer and pumice away the raised texture. Brush with a brass brush and dish soap.

FIG. 02

Key

Lay the key on a steel bench block and use a center punch and mallet to mark the center of the key where you want a hole. Drill the hole using a ¹⁄₁₆-inch drill bit and dremel tool (FIG. 02). Enlarge the hole by drilling again with a ³⁄₁₆-inch bit. Your key may be different and require some adjustments in terms of drill bits. If you don't want to drill the key, you can always attach the center link with a jump ring.

Charms

Use heavy-duty wire cutters to remove the shanks from the buttons. Use a multipurpose adhesive to glue the rivoli crystal and vintage buttons

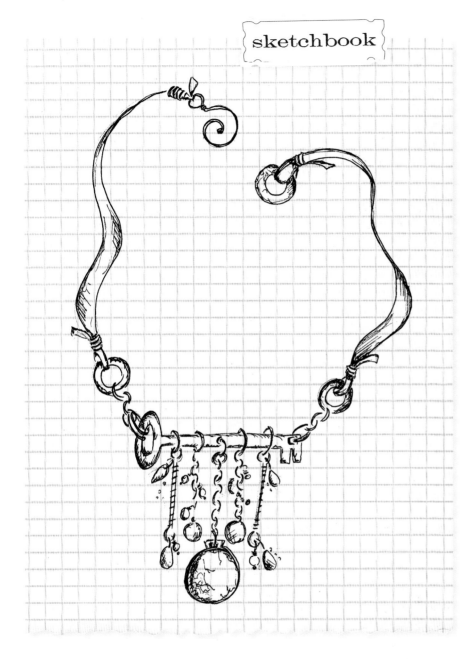

Coil Beads
Create six coil beads by wrapping wire around a mandrel (FIG. 05) and cutting them into ⅜-inch (1 cm) lengths.

FIG.05

Oxidize
Dip the silver-plated chain and the 10-mm copper jump rings in a liver of sulfur solution to oxidize. Pumice to reveal a little of the copper base metal and/or brush with a brass brush and dish soap to shine it.

create the links
Use the detail photo on page 104 as a guide while you work.

Center Link
String one gunmetal bead cap, a sapphire crystal, and a bead cap onto a wire and finish each end with a wrapped loop—connect the heart link to one of the loops before wrapping. Attach the locket at the opposite end with a 6-mm jump ring. Connect the heart link to the hole in the key with a 10-mm jump ring with the brass spacer bead hanging in front.

Chain Link
Cut a seven-link section of chain. Connect a button or crystal charm to the end of the chain with a 6-mm jump ring. String one purple and gold glass bead and a gunmetal bead cap onto a balled head pin

to the charms (FIG. 03).

Wire Links
Cut a piece of wire 2 inches (5.1 cm) long and make a loop on each end. Texture the link

FIG.03

with the chasing hammer (FIG. 04). Repeat to make a second wire link.

FIG.04

and finish with a wrapped loop. Attach this three links above the button charm with a 6-mm jump ring. String a sapphire crystal, a bead cap, and a silver crystal onto a head pin, finish with a wrapped loop, and attach it two links above the last dangle with a 6-mm jump ring. String a gunmetal bead, a brown glass spacer, and a gunmetal bead cap onto a head pin and finish with a wrapped loop. Attach this piece to the top link of the chain with a 6-mm jump ring. Repeat to create a second section of chain with dangles. Hang one dangle to the right and one to the left of the locket dangle with a 10-mm jump ring.

Wire Link

String one purple and gold glass bead and a gunmetal bead cap onto a balled head pin and finish with a wrapped loop. Connect this to the bottom loop on one wire link with a 3-mm jump ring. Hang a crystal drop on the top and bottom loops of the link with 5-mm jump rings. Repeat to make a second wire dangle. Connect the links on the outside of the chain dangles with 10-mm jump rings.

string the necklace

1 Cut two three-link sections of chain. Connect each side of the key to the 9-mm copper links, attach the copper links to the sections of chain, and attach the ends of the chains to another 9-mm copper link. Connect the copper links to two of the textured copper washers (FIG. 06).

FIG.06

FIG.07

2 Cut the ribbons in half. Thread two ribbons (one of each color) through a textured washer and double over. Twist the ends of the ribbon through three coil beads, spacing them approximately 2 inches (5.1 cm) apart.

3 Tie one end of the ribbon to a hook clasp and the other end to the third washer and attach the third button charm to the clasp. You can also add a dot of fabric adhesive to the knots to make sure they are extra secure (FIG. 07).

stone's throw

You can use whatever chain scraps you have to make this necklace. Link them together with jump rings and heavy links of chain to create a random-looking effect.

COLLECT

5 tumbled blue stone
beads, 40 x 20 mm

27 inches (68.6 cm) of
elongated silver base
metal chain, 4 x 2 mm

9 inches (22.9 cm) of base
metal chain, 9 mm

36 inches (91.4 cm) of
elongated silver base
metal chain, 4 x 3 mm

12 inches (30.5 cm) of
49-strand .024-inch
(.61 mm) beading wire

2 silver base metal jump
rings, 4 mm

Silver base metal jump
ring, 6 mm

2 crimp bead findings

Silver base metal S-hook
clasp, 22 mm

INSTRUMENTS

Wire cutters
Chain-nose pliers
Small screwdriver

TECHNIQUES

Opening and closing
a jump ring
Crimping

DIMENSIONS

24 inches (61 cm)

methodology
link the chains

Side #1

Cut a 6½-inch (16.5 cm) section
of chain from each kind of chain.
Link the smallest chain to the large
chain with a 4-mm silver jump ring.
Open the large link of chain and
attach the medium elongated chain.
At the opposite end attach the two
smaller chains to the large chain
with a 4-mm jump ring.

Side #2

1 Split the medium elongated
chain into six sections measuring 1½ inches (3.8 cm) and three sections measuring 2¾ inches (7 cm).

2 Attach a five-link section of
9-mm chain to three 1½-inch
(3.8 cm) sections. Use a single
9-mm link to connect the ends of
these three chains and the remaining three 1½-inch (3.8 cm) sections.

3 Attach a four-link section of
9-mm chain to the three pieces
of chain. At the opposite end attach
the 2¾-inch (7 cm) pieces of chain.
Connect the ends of the chain with a
6-mm jump ring (FIG. 01).

FIG.01

string the stones

1 Make a loop at the end of the
beading wire and secure with a
crimp finding (FIG. 02).

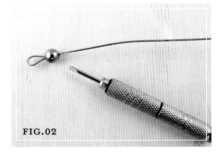

FIG.02

2 Split the remaining small
elongated chain in half and
string the end link on both of these
chains onto the wire followed by a
blue stone bead (FIG. 03).

FIG.03

3 Wrap the chain snugly around the stone and string the links that match up the most closely on both chains (FIG. 04). Repeat until you have used all the stones and finish the end as you did when you started (FIG. 05).

FIG.04

FIG.05

4 Connect a beading wire loop to the jump ring on side 1 and the other beading wire loop to the jump ring on side 2.

5 Attach a clasp to the end of the chains (FIG. 06).

FIG.06

sketchbook

streets of bombay

This piece evokes the photos I've seen of India. Brass deities, colorful saris, sparkly gems ... I hope to go see for myself someday!

methodology

1 Using chain-nose pliers, split the ball chain into one 10-link section and one 13-link section.

2 String a seed bead and a round 5 x 1.5-mm garnet onto the nylon cord. String this pattern three more times and tie around the link in between the balls on the chain (FIG. 01). Repeat to string a loop of four garnets between nine balls on the 10-link chain and 12 balls on the 13-link chain. You may want to secure each knot with a dot of adhesive.

FIG.01

FIG.02

3 Secure 10 inches (25.4 cm) of beading wire to each end of each chain with a crimp bead (FIG. 02).

FIG.03

4 Thread each of the wires through a bead cone (FIG. 03).

FIG.04

5 Working each side at the same time and each wire separately, string one brass spacer, a black bicone, a brass spacer, a diamond garnet, a faceted garnet, a diamond garnet, and a seed bead (FIG. 04). Thread both wires together through a paisley bead (FIG. 05).

6 Again working both sides at the same time and each wire separately, string one diamond

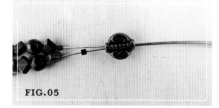
FIG.05

garnet, a faceted garnet, a diamond garnet, a brass spacer, a black bicone, a brass spacer, a diamond garnet, a faceted garnet, a diamond garnet, and a seed bead and pass both wires together through a paisley bead (FIG. 06).

FIG.06

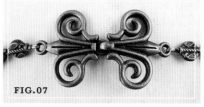
FIG.07

7 Repeat step 6, and then secure the ends of the wires to the clasp with a crimp bead (FIG. 07).

danio

Modern black-and-white beads suspended from silver wires led me to a minimalist thought: zebrafish. A tropical freshwater fish well suited for aquariums, the *Danio rerio* is commonly sold under the name zebra danio.

COLLECT

14 black round crystals, 4 mm

28 silver spacer beads, 3 mm

7 black and white shell beads, 20 mm

18 inches (45.7 cm) of black rubber tubing, 1.6 mm

25 inches (63.5 cm) of 20-gauge fine silver half-hard wire

Steel neck ring cable, 16 inches (40.6 cm) long

2 memory wire square silver glue-in findings

Silver lobster clasp, 10 mm

2 silver jump rings, 5 mm

Multipurpose adhesive

INSTRUMENTS

Scissors
Wire cutters
Butane torch
Steel bench block
Chasing hammer
Round-nose pliers
Third-hand tweezers

TECHNIQUES

Using a torch/balling up wire
Hammering
Simple loop

DIMENSIONS

19.5 inches (49.5 cm)

methodology

cut the tubing

1 Cut two sections of rubber tubing, each 7 inches (17.8 cm) long.

2 Cut six more pieces, each ½ inch (1.3 cm) long (FIG. 01).

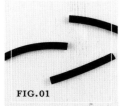

FIG.01

create the beaded dangles

1 Cut the wire into seven pieces: two at 2¾ inches (7 cm), two at 3¼ inches (8.3 cm), two at 2½ inches (6.4 cm), and one at 3½ inches (8.9 cm) long.

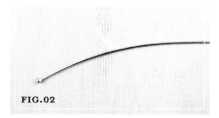

FIG.02

2 Ball up one end of each of the wires with a torch (FIG. 02). If you don't have a torch you can always make a tiny hook at the end of each wire.

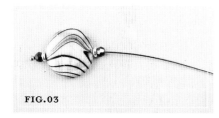

FIG.03

3 String a crystal, a silver spacer, a shell bead, a silver spacer, and a crystal onto each wire (FIG. 03).

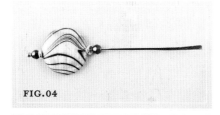

FIG.04

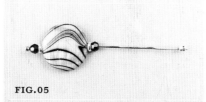

FIG.05

4 On a steel bench block, hammer the end of the wire just above the crystal bead to flatten it (FIG. 04).

5 Finish each end with a loop, making sure the loop is perpendicular to the wire (FIG. 05). The finished dangle lengths are two at 2¼ inches (5.7 cm), two at 2¾ inches (7 cm), two at 2 inches (5.1 cm), and one at 3 inches (7.5 cm).

EXPERIMENT
Any large, graphic bead could look great with this modern design. Try chunky round faceted gemstones or flat silver ovals with a matte finish. Ooh, how about big felt balls?

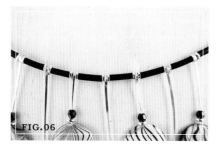

FIG.06

string the necklace

1 String one 7-inch (17.8 cm) piece of tubing onto the cable followed by a spacer bead, the 2 ¼-inch (5.7 cm) dangle, a spacer bead, and a short piece of tubing (FIG. 06). Repeat this sequence, stringing the dangles in this size order: 2¾ inches (7 cm), 2 inches (5.1 cm), and 3 inches (7.5 cm). Repeat for the opposite side.

FIG.07

FIG.08

2 Finish the ends of the necklace by gluing the end findings to the cable (FIG. 07). Attach the clasp to each end with jump rings (FIG. 08).

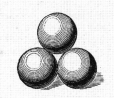

COLLECT

74 multicolored felt balls

4 yards (3.6 m) of black elastic, 1.5 mm

Wooden ring, 1¾ inches (4.4 cm) in diameter

Wool felt in desired colors

Sewing thread in desired colors

INSTRUMENTS

Awl

Tapestry needle

Measuring tape

Scissors

Lighter

Adhesive

Sewing needle

TECHNIQUES

Knotting

Hand sewing

DIMENSIONS

29 inches (73.7 cm) long

Playful is the only word I can use to describe this piece. It makes me think of children popping out of ball pools, bright red gumball-filled machines, and air-mix lottery machines with balls shooting around inside!

gumballs

methodology
create the felt ball pieces

1 Use an awl to poke a hole through the top of each felt ball (FIG. 01). Thread a tapestry needle with the elastic (FIG. 02).

FIG.01

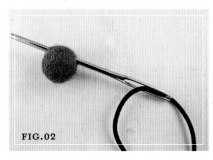

FIG.02

2 String the felt balls onto the elastic in any order.

3 Tie a knot around the first felt ball. Move down approximately 2 inches (5.1 cm) and tie another knot around the second felt ball. Cut the elastic between the second and the third balls (FIG. 03).

FIG.03

4 For added security, you can burn the ends of your elastic (I recommend doing this outdoors or in a well-ventilated area) or add a drop of adhesive to the knot. Re-

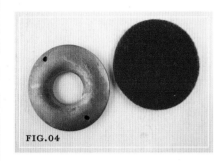
FIG.04

peat 36 more times to make a total of 37 two-ball sections.

create the closure ring

1 From the wool felt, cut a circle just slightly bigger than the wooden ring and glue to one side of the ring (FIG. 04). Repeat for the opposite side and trim away the excess.

2 Thread the sewing needle with your desired color of thread. Anchor the sewing thread with two forward stitches and one backstitch, and whipstitch around each felt piece, skimming the surface of the felt (FIG. 05). You can create whatever pattern you like (FIG. 06).

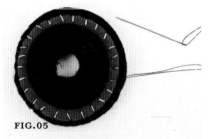
FIG.05

FIG.06

assemble the necklace

1 Cut two pieces of elastic 44 inches (1.2 m) long, place them side by side, and fold them in half.

2 Starting at the fold, tie the felt ball pieces in knots around the two strands of elastic. Leave approximately ¾ inch (1.9 cm) in between each felt ball dangle.

3 Continue knotting felt ball dangles down 13 inches (33 cm) on each side.

4 Tie one felt ball really close to the elastic (FIG. 07). On the opposite side, thread the elastic through the felted ring and knot (FIG. 08).

5 Leave a little space and continue knotting felt ball pieces down the front.

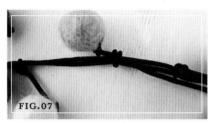
FIG.07

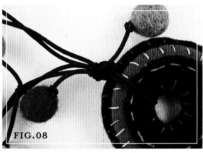
FIG.08

VARIATION

EXPERIMENT
It's easy to wear the necklace in different lengths because you can clasp any of the balls into the closure ring.

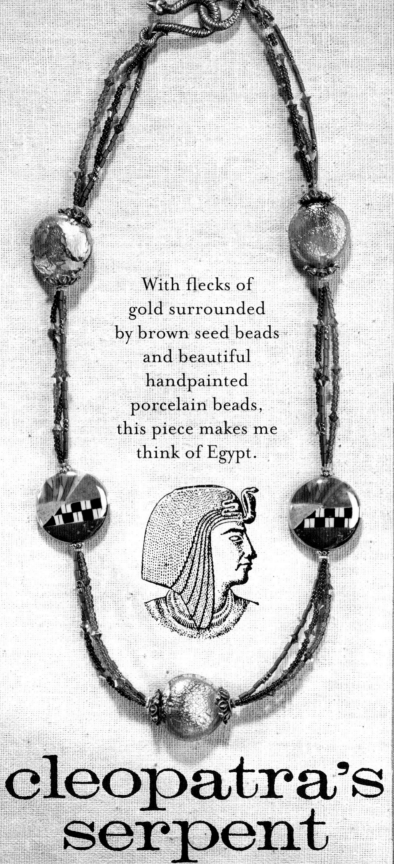

With flecks of
gold surrounded
by brown seed beads
and beautiful
handpainted
porcelain beads,
this piece makes me
think of Egypt.

cleopatra's serpent

COLLECT

Amber seed beads, 3 grams
Brown tube beads, 3 grams
Silver seed beads, 1 gram
Brown seed beads, 3 grams
Copper seed beads,
    0.5 gram
42 bicone Swarovski
    crystals, 4 mm
10 brass spacer beads, 4 mm
6 brass bead caps, 12 mm
4 brass bead caps, 5 mm
3 Venetian glass beads,
    20 mm
2 handpainted porcelain
    beads, 25 mm
69 inches (1.8 m) of 7-strand
    .015-inch (.38 mm) gold
    beading wire
6 brass crimp beads
6 brass wire guards
Brass snake clasp, 28 mm
2 brass jump rings, 6 mm

EXTENDER

18 Crystal Copper Swarovski
    helix crystals, 8 x 8 mm
5 gold with foil glass beads,
    11 mm
24 brass spacer beads, 4 mm
13 inches (33 cm) of 7-strand
    .015-inch (.38 mm) gold
    beading wire
2 brass crimp beads
Brass lobster clasp,
    5 x 17 mm
Brass jump ring, 10 mm

INSTRUMENTS

Tape measure
Wire cutters
Crimping pliers
Round-nose pliers

TECHNIQUES

Crimping
Opening and closing
    a jump ring

DIMENSIONS

21.5 inches (54.6 cm) long

methodology
create the strands

1 Cut three strands of beading wire 23 inches (58.4 cm) long. Thread each of the ends through a crimp bead and a wire guard and then back through the crimp bead. Crimp.

2 Referring to FIG. 01 as you work, string 2⅛ inches (5.39 cm) of seed beads onto each strand:

Strand 1 (amber seed beads)
String ½ inch (1.3 cm) of seed beads, a crystal, ⅜ inch (1 cm) of seed beads, a crystal, ½ (1.3 cm) of seed beads, a crystal, and ⅜ inch (1 cm) of seed beads.

Strand 2 (brown tube beads)
String three brown tube beads, a silver seed bead, a copper seed bead, a silver seed bead, four brown tube beads, a crystal, four brown tube beads, a silver seed bead, a copper seed bead, a silver seed bead, and three brown tube beads.

Strand 3 (brown seed beads)
String ⅜ inch (1 cm) of seed beads, a crystal, ⅜ (1 cm) of seed beads, a crystal, ½ (1.3 cm) of seed beads, a crystal, and ⅜ inch (1 cm) of seed beads.

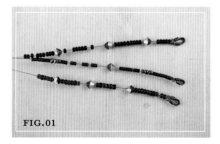

FIG.01

3 String one 4-mm brass spacer, a 12-mm bead cap, a Venetian glass bead, a 12-mm bead cap, and a 4-mm brass spacer onto all three strands (FIG. 02).

FIG.02

4 Repeat the seed bead sequences from step 2 to create three side-by-side strands.

5 String one 4-mm brass spacer, a 5-mm bead cap, a porcelain bead, a 5-mm bead cap, and a 4-mm brass spacer onto all three strands (FIG. 03).

FIG.03

6 Repeat all the seed bead sequences from step 2 and the Venetian bead sequence from step 3.

7 String the other side of the necklace so it mirrors the first half.

finish the ends

1 Thread each of the wires through a crimp bead and the wire guards and back through the crimp bead. Crimp.

2 Attach the clasp with 6-mm jump rings (FIG. 04).

extender

1 String a 4-mm brass spacer, a helix crystal, a 4-mm brass spacer, a helix crystal, a 4-mm brass spacer, a helix crystal,

FIG. 04

a 4-mm brass spacer, and a gold bead onto the 13 inches (33 cm) of beading wire. Continue this pattern until you've used all the helix crystals (FIG. 05).

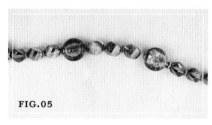

FIG. 05

2 String a crimp bead onto each side, thread the clasp onto one wire and the jump ring onto the other, pass back through the crimp beads, and crimp (FIG. 06).

FIG. 06

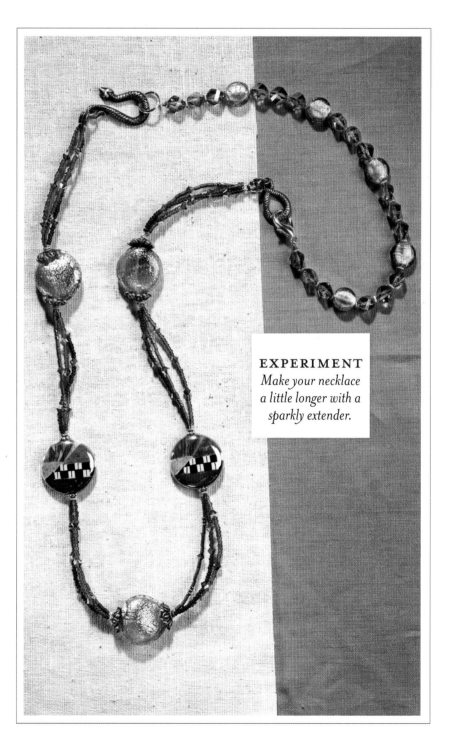

EXPERIMENT
Make your necklace a little longer with a sparkly extender.

mountains of tibet

COLLECT

9 oval wooden beads,
   13 x 25 mm
1 oval wooden bead,
   18 x 55 mm
Copper seed beads,
   1 gram
40 copper bead caps,
   7 mm
10 freeform faceted
   green agate beads,
   38 mm
20 silver bead caps,
   13.5 mm
2 yards (1.8 m) of re-
   cycled silk ribbon,
   ⅝ inch (1.6 cm) wide
Metallic thread in cop-
   per and mint
3 yards (2.7 m) of bur-
   gundy nylon cord
Adhesive

INSTRUMENTS

Tapestry needle
Sewing needle
Large-hole needle
Scissors
Metal hole punch

TECHNIQUES

Punching holes

DIMENSIONS

29 inches (73.7 cm)

With many of the tallest mountains on the planet, Tibet is often called "the roof of the world." The free-form cut stones in this necklace, coupled with the bright silk, remind me of the scenery you might find in Tibet's very special landscape.

methodology
create the ribbon beads

1 Thread a tapestry needle with the silk ribbon. Poke the needle through the center of one of the wooden beads, positioning the ribbon flat against the bead, and wrap the ribbon around the bead. Trim the ends of the ribbon, leaving ¼ inch (6 mm); add a dot of glue to the ends and tuck them inside the bead (FIG. 01). Repeat for the other beads.

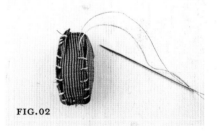

FIG. 02

2 Embellish the surface of the beads with thread and seed beads. Thread a sewing needle with two strands of metallic thread in copper and mint. Anchor the thread on the surface of the bead with two forward stitches and one backstitch. Sew a desired pattern onto the bead and tie off the thread as you did when you started (FIG. 02). Seed beads can be added to the centers of the Xs in the

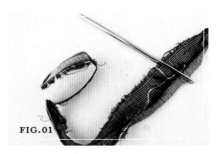

FIG. 01

*Notice how the silver bead
caps give a really finished
look to the ribbon beads.
When it comes to neck-
laces, never underestimate
the power of smaller findings to boost the impact of
your larger beads.*

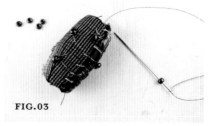

same way with thread (FIG. 03).
Repeat for each wooden bead.

string the necklace

Note You may have trouble threading the nylon cord through the bead
caps. I used a hole punch tool to
open the holes in the metal beads
just a little. Don't worry if they
aren't perfect because the knots
and other beads will hide the holes
(FIG. 04).

FIG.04

1 Cut two strands of nylon cord
4 feet (1.2 m) long and knot together at the ends, leaving a 6-inch
(15.2 cm) tail. Thread the opposite
ends onto a large-hole needle.

2 String one copper bead cap, an
agate bead, and a copper bead
cap. Make a knot with both strands
of nylon together and slide the knot
up against the stone. Here's a good
trick: Once you make the knot,
leave the opening a little loose, put
the end of the needle in the loop,

and slide the knot up against the
bead (FIG. 05).

FIG.05

3 String one copper bead cap, a
silver bead cap, a ribbon bead,
a silver bead cap, and a copper bead
cap onto the nylon and follow with
a knot (FIG. 06).

FIG.06

4 Repeat, alternating the stone
and ribbon bead sequence.
Tie the ends in a snug knot, secure
with a drop of glue, and trim the
ends (FIG. 07).

FIG.07

afternoon
tea

Mom held tea parties for my sister and me throughout our childhood. I can still remember the small table she had hand-painted with pink hearts and the aroma of real tea as we poured it into dainty porcelain cups.

COLLECT

Copper seed beads,
  2 grams

5 pink carved tulip beads,
  6 x 4 mm

49 fire-polished faceted
  pink Czech beads, 4 mm

73 copper daisy spacers,
  5 mm

17 fuchsia freshwater
  pearls, 4 x 6 mm

20 round pink glass
  beads, 5 mm

10 pink pearls, 8 mm

9 twisted copper beads,
  8 mm

11 Crystal Golden Shadow
  Swarovski crystals,
  8 x 6 mm

Copper bead cone,
  15 x 10 mm

10 shell leaf links,
  14 x 24 mm

Fabric rose link, 2 inches
  (5.1 cm)

Copper bird locket, 33 mm

Shell charm, 12 mm

45 inches (1.1 m) of
  19-strand .015-inch
  (.38 mm) copper
  beading wire

36 inches (91 cm) of
  20-gauge copper wire

6 copper crimp beads

Four 18-gauge copper jump
  rings, 6 mm

20 copper jump rings or
  chain links, 9 mm

One 18-gauge copper
  jump ring, 10 mm

Copper toggle clasp, 16 mm

Lace scraps, 8 inches
  (20.3 cm) total

INSTRUMENTS

Wire cutters
Round-nose pliers

TECHNIQUES

Wrapped loop

DIMENSIONS

32 inches (81.3 cm)

methodology
string the beads

As you work this section, follow along with FIG. 01.

FIG. 01

Strand # 1 (pink tulips)

String three seed beads, a tulip, three seed beads, a pink Czech bead, three seed beads, a daisy spacer, a fuchsia freshwater pearl, and a daisy spacer onto the beading wire. Repeat this pattern until the beading measures 10 inches (25.4 cm), ending with three seed beads.

Strand # 2 (crystals)

String a pink glass bead, a daisy spacer, a pink pearl, a daisy spacer, a pink glass bead, and a twisted copper bead onto the beading wire. Continue this sequence eight more times *except* alternate between crystals and pearls. String one pink glass bead, a daisy spacer, a pearl, a daisy spacer, and a pink glass bead onto the wire.

Strand # 3 (Czech beads)

1 String one Czech bead, a daisy spacer, a Czech bead, a seed bead, a Czech bead, a daisy spacer, a fuchsia freshwater pearl, and a daisy spacer onto the beading wire.

2 String on five Czech beads separated by seed beads, then a daisy spacer, a pink pearl, and a daisy spacer. Continue this sequence six more times. Finish with a Czech bead.

FIG. 02

3 Cut a piece of wire 2½ inches (6.4 cm) long and finish the end with a wrapped loop. Secure one end of each of the beaded strands to the wrapped loop with crimp beads (FIG. 02). Secure the opposite ends of the strands to a 6-mm jump ring using crimp beads.

FIG. 03

4 Thread the wire through a copper bead cone. String a crystal and a daisy spacer and finish with a wrapped loop (FIG. 03).

make the links

1 Make a wrapped loop on one end of the copper wire. String a crystal onto the wire and finish with a wrapped loop. Repeat to make another beaded link with a pearl. Repeat to make three more crystal links and three more pearl links (FIG. 04).

2 Connect a leaf link to the bead cone side of the necklace with

FIG. 04

FIG.05

a 9-mm jump ring. Connect a crystal bead link to the opposite side of the leaf link with a 9-mm jump ring. Connect another leaf link on the other side with another 9-mm jump ring. Repeat, alternating a pearl link, a crystal link, and a pearl link between the leaf links, ending with a leaf link (FIG. 05).

create the rose cluster

1 I cut the beads that were on the original rose and sewed ones that matched the necklace in their place. Do the same.

2 Attach the bead strands to the link on the rose with a 9-mm jump ring.

3 Attach the locket with the 10-mm jump ring to the 9-mm jump ring.

4 String a pink pearl onto a piece of copper wire and finish each end with a wrapped loop, connecting the shell charm on one end. Attach it to the 9-mm jump ring with a 6-mm jump ring.

FIG.06

5 Cut scraps of lace and tie one piece to the locket's jump ring. Tie a second piece to a 9-mm jump ring and attach it to the locket (FIG. 06).

6 Connect a leaf link to the opposite side of the rose link. Connect a crystal link to the opposite side of the leaf link. Repeat to mirror the other side.

7 Finish the ends with a toggle clasp connected to the leaf links with 6-mm copper jump rings (FIG. 07).

FIG.07

Both the long jasper tubes and the tiny faceted carnelian beads used in this design are a form of chalcedony. Because of its abundance, chalcedony was undoubtedly one of the first raw materials used by early humans. Due to the stone's beauty, the leap from tool to jewel didn't take long.

chalcedony

methodology

1 Cut 18 sections of chain each 2½ inches (6.4 cm) long.

2 String one gold bead cap, one tube bead, and a second bead cap onto the gold wire, start a wrapped loop on each end, attach two sections of chain to each loop, then close the loops (FIG. 01).

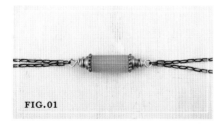

FIG.01

3 Repeat step 1 to connect the remaining 14 sections of chain to 8 more beaded links to form the necklace.

4 String a small carnelian bead onto a head pin and finish with a wrapped loop. Repeat 17 more times.

5 String a yellow pearl and a brass spacer bead onto a head pin and finish with a wrapped loop. Repeat 8 times (FIG. 02).

FIG.02

6 Attach a pearl and a leaf charm to each pair of chain sections with jump rings. Repeat, adding a carnelian dangle on the top and bottom sections of the chain (FIG. 03).

FIG.03

COLLECT

8 brass flower spacer beads

4 pink pressed-glass rose beads, 18 mm

8 faceted pineapple quartz beads, 14 x 10 mm

8 round brass beads, 5 mm

7 pink milk glass beads, 15 mm

2 round pink beads, 8 mm

3 brass charms in garden theme, 15 to 20 mm

12 inches (30.5 cm) of 20-gauge brass wire

20 inches (50.8 cm) of 49-strand .018-inch (.46 m) gold beading wire

Five 8-inch (20.3 cm) strands of commercial bead chain in yellow

Two 8-inch (20.3 cm) strands of commercial bead chain in pink

2 butterfly chandelier components, 30 x 30 mm

2 enamel link components, 20 x 50 mm

6 brass crimp beads

2 brass wire guards

Brass leaf toggle clasp, 40 mm

13 brass jump rings, 5 mm

5 brass head pins

INSTRUMENTS

Wire cutters
Round-nose pliers
Crimping pliers
Chain-nose pliers

TECHNIQUES

Wrapped loop
Crimping
Opening and closing a jump ring

DIMENSIONS

28 inches (71.1 cm)

Butterflies, birds, and blossoms—this necklace incorporates the best of early summer days.

english garden

methodology

1 String one flower spacer bead, a pink rose bead, and a flower spacer bead onto the brass wire. Connect one end to a butterfly chandelier component and the opposite end to an enamel link component with wrapped loops (FIG. 01). Repeat to make a pair.

FIG. 01

2 String one crimp bead onto the end of the beading wire. String the wire guard through the enamel link and thread the wire through the guard and back through the crimp bead. Secure the

sketchbook

FIG.03

by one end of the clasp, threading the end of the wire back through the crimp beads. Remove the slack from the strand. Use chain-nose pliers to flatten the crimp beads (FIG. 03). Repeat for the other piece.

5 Use the jump rings to connect the yellow beaded chain to the butterfly components. The pink strands get attached to the second and fourth links on the components (FIG. 04).

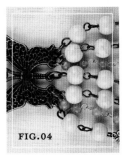

FIG.04

6 String each of the remaining three pink glass beads and the two 8-mm pink beads onto a head pin and finish with a wrapped loop. Attach the garden charms with 5-mm jump rings sporadically along the beaded chain sections. Open a link on the beaded chain to attach the pink bead dangles (FIG. 05).

wire by crimping (FIG. 02). Cut the wire from the spool, leaving 6 inches (15.2 cm). Repeat for the other piece.

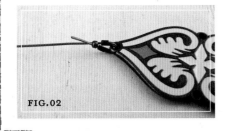

FIG.02

3 String one quartz bead, a round brass bead, a pink milk glass bead, a round brass bead, a quartz bead, a flower spacer, a pink rose bead, a flower spacer, a quartz bead, a round brass bead, a pink milk glass bead, a round brass bead, and a quartz bead onto the beading wire. Repeat for the other piece.

4 Trim the end of the wire, leaving 1 inch (2.5 cm). String two crimp beads followed

FIG.05

kelp forest

The seed beads used in this piece came from an attic of sorts in my grandmother's house. Imagine a tin filled with buttons, river stones, and tangled hanks of seed beads. Thanks to my sweet dad for rescuing the tin! Because these are vintage seed beads, they're not uniform in size, so the daisy chains aren't perfect—they're whimsical.

COLLECT

Seed beads in desired
   colors and sizes
Decorative chain
Jump rings
Beading thread
Instruments
Wire cutters
Round-nose pliers
Scissors
Collapsible beading
   needle
Chain-nose pliers

TECHNIQUES

Opening and closing a
   jump ring

DIMENSIONS

48 inches (121.9 cm) long

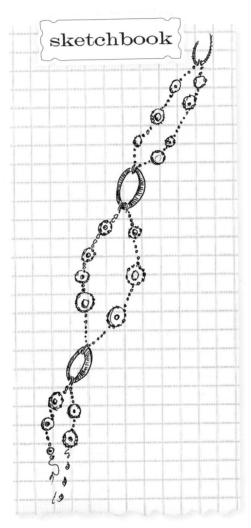

sketchbook

methodology

prepare the chain

Break the decorative chain into three link sections, leaving a jump ring on each end.

make the daisy chain

1 Cut a piece of beading thread 18 inches (45.7 cm) long and tie it to one of the jump rings with a knot. Thread the filament with it onto a collapsible beading needle.

2 String five to 10 green seed beads onto the needle followed by an even number of colorful seed beads; this will be the flower petals around the center of the daisy (FIG. 01).

FIG.01

FIG.02

3 Pass the needle through the first colorful seed bead to create a ring and slide the ring up against the green beads (FIG. 02).

4 Drop your center bead into the ring to check the fit and make adjustments by increasing or decreasing the colorful seed beads.

5 String the center bead onto the needle and secure it by passing the needle through the bead on the opposite side of the ring (FIG. 03).

FIG.03

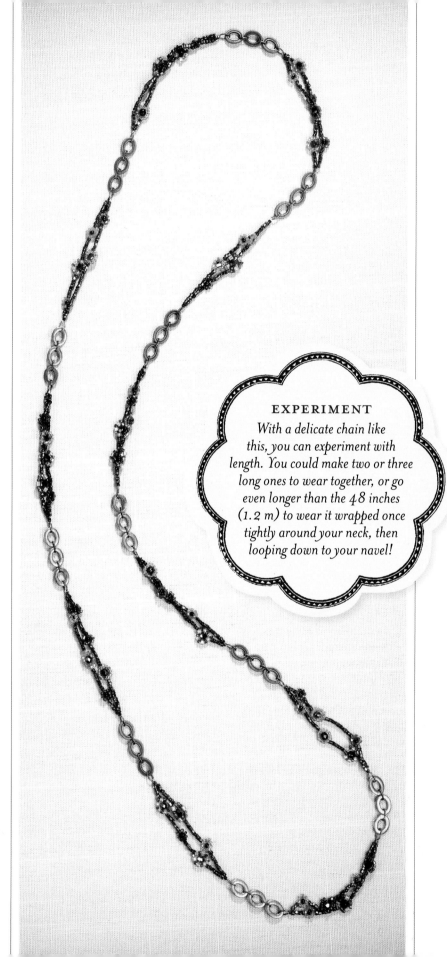

EXPERIMENT

With a delicate chain like this, you can experiment with length. You could make two or three long ones to wear together, or go even longer than the 48 inches (1.2 m) to wear it wrapped once tightly around your neck, then looping down to your navel!

FIG.04

6 String seven to 10 more green seed beads followed by another daisy. The beauty is that there is no right and wrong pattern, color, or length between daisy combinations here.

7 After three or four daisies, string a row of green seed beads and knot the thread to a jump ring on a second section of chain (FIG. 04). Pass the needle through the last row of green seed beads, then begin a separate strand.

8 Repeat steps 2 through 6 to make a second strand of seed beads, and then pass the needle through the last green seed bead on the other strand.

FIG.05

9 Tie off the filament (FIG. 05).

10 Repeat steps 1 through 9, creating as many daisy sections as you like and linking the sections of chain as you go.

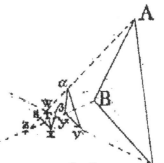

With their clean yet organic feel, the elements of this piece make me think of doors, casements, bull's-eye windows, and other elements of architecture.

geometry

methodology
embellish the rectangular beads

1 Sand each of the large rectangular bead's edges with sandpaper to remove some of the varnish.

2 Paint the inside of the frames pink and the outside edge gold (FIG. 01).

FIG. 01

3 Burn lines into the sides of the wooden rectangles with a wood-burning tool (FIG. 02).

FIG. 02

4 If desired, seal the beads with a clear acrylic varnish.

sketchbook

FIG.04

opposite side, string another glass spacer, and finish both ends with a wrapped loop (FIG. 04). Repeat two more times.

3 Apply a liver of sulfur patina to the silver-plated oval links (FIG. 05).

FIG.05

link together

1 Cut a portion of the gunmetal chain into several single links and several double links. Link the three large rectangle beads together with single links of chain. On both ends of this section link two links of chain, an oval link, and two links of chain, then connect a shell link with a jump ring.

2 On each side of a square bead, connect two links of chain, an oval link, two links of chain, a shell link, two links of chain, and a square bead.

3 Connect both of the linked sections together with 6-inch (15.2 cm) pieces of chain.

make the links

1 String one flower spacer and one wooden rectangle onto the wire. Then string a garnet, a silver spacer, a garnet, a silver spacer, and

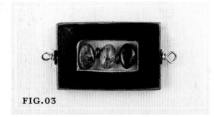

FIG.03

a garnet so they sit in the middle of the rectangle. Bring the wire out to the opposite side, string another flower spacer, and finish both ends with a wrapped loop (FIG. 03). Repeat two more times.

2 String one glass spacer bead and a square donut bead onto the wire. Then string a flower spacer, a jasper bead, and a flower spacer so they sit in the center. Bring the wire out to the

Macramé was one
of my first forms of
jewelry making.
Fifteen years later,
it's the same square
knot with a twist,
used here for a
wraparound necklace
in blue hemp.

peace dreams

COLLECT

Shell button, 20 mm

Brass peace sign, 14 mm

40 silver spacer beads,
   1 x 5 mm

20 purple dyed jasper
   beads, 8 x 12 mm

72 silver beads,
   2 x 5 mm

6 yards (5.4 m) of blue
   hemp cord, run
   through a beeswax
   block to smooth

INSTRUMENTS

Scissors

Crochet hook, any size

TECHNIQUE

Macramé

DIMENSIONS

37 inches (94.1 cm)

methodology

1 Cut a piece of hemp 80 inches (2 m) long and fold it in half. String the button from the back side to the front followed by the peace sign. Place the tail back through the opposite hole and even up the two tails, pulling the peace sign snugly against the button (FIG. 01).

FIG.01

2 With the right tail, make four half-hitch knots (FIG. 02). Pull the right tail across the top of the left so there is a loop, and thread the end of the right tail up from the bottom through the loop, sliding the knot down toward the button.

FIG.02

3 Cut a second piece of hemp 8 feet (2.4 m) long and fold in half. Tie this piece just below the half-hitch knot.

4 Lay the right tail on top of the center strands while the left tail goes over the top of the right tail, then back behind the center strands and through the loop

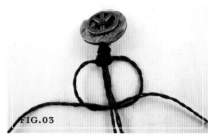

FIG.03

made by the right tail (FIG. 03). Pull snug, sliding the knot down toward the button.

5 Repeat step 4, except this time lay the left tail on top of the center strands with the right tail going on top, then behind the center strands and up through the loop made by the left tail (FIG. 04). Pull snug. This completes one full square knot.

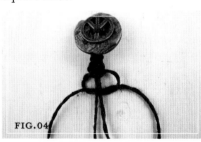

FIG.04

FIG.05

FIG.07

FIG.10

6 Repeat steps 4 and 5 one more time to make a second full square knot.

7 String one silver spacer, a purple bead, and a silver spacer onto the two center strands. Bring the outside tails down and around and make two full square knots (FIG. 05).

8 String a silver bead onto all four tails. Reverse the outside tails with the inside tails and, leaving a little space, make five full knots (FIG. 06).

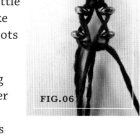

FIG.06

9 String a silver bead onto all four tails again; make two full knots; string a silver spacer, a purple bead, and a silver spacer onto the center tails; and make two full knots followed by the silver bead sequence. Repeat this pattern for 16½ inches (41.9 cm).

10 Make five full knots. String one silver spacer, a purple bead, and a silver spacer onto the two center strands. Make two full knots and string two silver beads onto the outside tails, leaving them on the side while you make two more full knots (FIG. 07). Continue this pattern for 18 inches (45.7 cm).

11 Finish the end by making a 2-inch (5.1 cm) section with half-hitch knots (FIG. 08). Loop the end around to make a loop for the button, pulling the tails through the first knot with a crochet hook (FIG. 09).

FIG.08

FIG.09

12 Wrap the extra cord around and knot twice. Trim the excess. Place the button through the loop to close (FIG. 10).

EXPERIMENT

Although this project is in the ropes chapter, don't be afraid to wrap it around your neck twice to wear it as a choker. If you want to wear Peace Dreams this way, check the length while you're making the necklace and customize it to fit you perfectly.

pontocho

I've always loved kimono fabric and was just thrilled to find this cording. Pontocho is a district of Kyoto known for its tea houses, geisha, and nightlife. Be the life of the party in this Japanese-themed necklace.

COLLECT

60 brass twisted spacer
  beads, 5 mm
16 blue goldstone ovals,
  6 x 4 mm
3 gold-filled twisted corrugated
  Hogan beads, 7.7 mm
44 gold-lined clear Czech
  faceted beads, 5 mm
19 faceted round amethyst
  beads, 6 mm
5 blue goldstone cubes,
  4 x 4 mm
10 clear Czech twisted beads,
  9 x 13 mm
6 transparent pink side-drilled
  Czech leaf beads, 14 x 9 mm
20 brass spacer beads, 5 mm
Faux ivory butterfly
  pendant, 35 mm
15 inches (38.1 cm) of 9-strand
  .015-inch (.38 mm) blue
  beading wire
2 yards (1.8 m) of brass open
  extender chain, 5 mm
2 yards (1.8 m) of 20-gauge
  brass wire
45 inches (1.1 m) of kimono cord
15 inches (38.1 cm) of nylon cord
4 brass crimp beads
Pressure-fit three-loop clasp,
  7 mm
2 brass lobster clasps, 10 mm
9 brass jump rings, 5 mm
2 base metal, yellow finish,
  fold-over cord findings,
  12.5 mm
Adhesive
Brown alcohol ink

INSTRUMENTS

Wire cutters
Crimping pliers
Round-nose pliers

TECHNIQUES

Crimping
Simple loop
Fold-over end loop
Alcohol inks

DIMENSIONS

Longest strand, 53 inches
  (1.3 m)

methodology
chain #1

1 String on one gold twisted spacer and a goldstone oval bead onto the beading wire. String a gold corrugated hogan bead and a goldstone oval, and repeat two more times. String a gold twisted spacer. Cut two, two-link sections of chain and attach one to each end of the beaded length with crimp beads.

2 String one 5-mm clear bead, a gold twisted spacer, an amethyst bead, a gold twisted spacer, and a 5-mm clear bead onto the brass wire and finish with a simple loop. Repeat 18 more times (even though we won't use them all on this chain).

3 Connect an amethyst link to each end of the two-link chain. Attach three links of chain to the opposite side of the amethyst beaded links. Repeat, alternating amethyst beaded links and three links of chain, using a total of four amethyst links on each side.

4 Attach 1¾ inches (4.4 cm) of chain to the last beaded link and connect to the first ring on the pressure-fit clasp with jump rings.

make the kimono strand & beaded bead

1 Cut the kimono cord so one piece measures 21 inches (53.3 cm) and the other 24 inches (61 cm). Finish one end on each kimono strand with fold-over ribbon end findings. Attach the lobster clasps to the loops with jump rings.

2 String a 5-mm clear bead, a gold twisted spacer bead, a goldstone cube, a gold twisted spacer bead, and a clear bead onto the center of the 15-inch (38.1 cm) nylon cord (FIG. 01).

FIG.01

3 On the right tail of the cord, string a gold twisted spacer bead, a goldstone cube, and a gold twisted spacer bead. Thread the left tail through the three beads in the opposite direction that the right tail is coming out. Pull the two tails, sliding the beads down to the center (FIG. 02).

FIG.02

4 String two clear beads onto both ends of the cord (FIG. 03). Repeat step 3.

FIG.03

5 Continue this pattern, repeating step 4 and then step 3, until you've used five cube beads.

6 Thread the left tail through the first beads to make a ring. Thread the kimono tail ends through

Take advantage of the fact that the kimono lariat is detachable by wearing it alone, without the beaded chains.

EXPERIMENT

If you know how to sew, you can make your own fabric-covered cording to get exactly the look you want. These instructions may not seem intuitive at first—just read through them first so you understand it all. Trust me, they work.

❶ Cut strips of fabric 2 inches (5.1 cm) wide on the bias and stitch them together end to end so you have a strip roughly 4 feet (1.2 m) long.

❷ Use rayon rat-tail cord (available in the notions section of the fabric store) as the cording. It's more slippery than cotton cord, which makes it easier to turn the cording inside out later. Cut a piece of rat-tail cord 8 feet (2.4 m) long. Mark the midpoint of the cord.

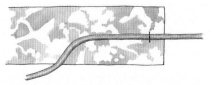

❸ Stitch the midpoint of the cord securely to the wrong side of the bias-cut strip, ½ inch (1.3 cm) from the end of the fabric and centered across its width (above).

❹ Flip the fabric so it's right-side up and fold it at the attachment point of the cord so half of the rat-tail lies against the right side of the fabric (below).

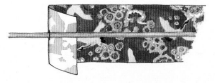

❺ With a cording foot on your sewing machine, and with the fabric strip folded lengthwise around the rat-tail, sew along the cord to encase it, starting your stitching at the end with the attachment stitching (below). Don't catch the cord in the stitching at any point. Trim the seams to reduce bulk.

❻ To turn the tube of fabric right side out, start at the end with the attachment stitching; use your thumb and index to work the fabric over the unexposed rat-tail cord, sliding the tube from the right half of the rat-tail over the left half (above). Cut off any exposed rat-tail.

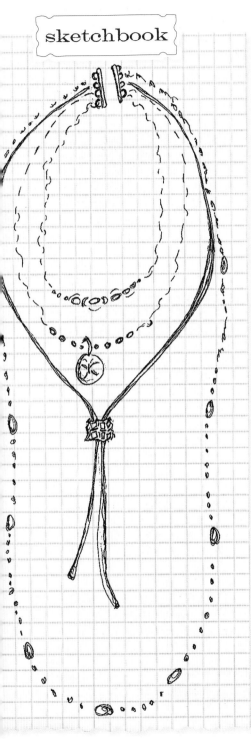

FIG.04

the beaded bead (FIG. 04). Weave the tails through the last beads, bringing the two tails together, and tie in a snug knot. Apply a dot of adhesive to secure the knot.

7 Connect a jump ring to the middle loop on each side of the pressure-fit clasp. The lobster clasps will hook onto these loops, creating a detachable necklace (FIG. 05).

FIG.05

chain #2

1 String a gold twisted spacer, an oval bead, a leaf bead, and a gold twisted spacer onto the beading wire. String a goldstone bead, a gold twisted spacer, a goldstone bead, a gold twisted spacer, and a leaf bead. Repeat that sequence, then follow with one goldstone bead, a gold twisted spacer, and the butterfly pendant. String the second half of the necklace so it mirrors the first.

2 Cut two pieces of chain 8½ inches (21.6 cm) long. Attach the ends of the necklace to the chain ends with crimp beads. Attach to the last link on the pressure-fit clasp with jump rings.

3 If desired, coat the

FIG.06

pendant with brown alcohol ink to highlight the texture (FIG. 06).

chain #3

1 String one brass spacer bead, a large clear twisted bead, and a brass spacer onto the brass wire and finish with a simple loop. Repeat nine more times.

2 Break the chain into 22 eight-link sections and connect all of the chains with alternating clear twisted bead and amethyst beaded links.

3 Connect the ends of the chain to the same jump rings on the last loop of the clasp (FIG. 07).

FIG.07

acknowledgments

To Lark Jewelry & Beading, thank you for publishing my work. I feel blessed to do what I love and it's possible through companies like yours. I am so proud to be a Lark author.

Nathalie Mornu, from acquisition to final details, you've been a gem to work with. Thank you for being patient with me, for making me laugh, and for giving positive feedback on my work.

Ray Hemachandra, thank you for encouraging my ideas and creativity. I appreciate all you do to support me, my fellow Lark authors, and the DIY jewelry world.

Kathy Holmes, fellow native Hoosier, you are always so nice to work with. Thank you for thinking my sketches are worthy of print. (I still can't believe they are!)

Much appreciation to editorial intern Ginny Roper, who helped keep everything organized.

Thank you, Linda Kopp, for being a good friend and editor of my first two books. I learned so much from you. You're one of the smartest gals I know—thank you for the constant love.

Stewart O'Shields, your photography is gorgeous. I love your attention to detail. Thank you for taking the time to make each of the necklaces shine.

Thank you, Karen Levy, super-human technical editor, for going over each and every word in this book to make sure that the bead counts matched the instructions and that the words were clear. Wow.

Alison McClure, Katie Hacker, Faith Harless, and Kellie Brace, without friends like you, books cannot be written. Thank you for coming to my studio and cheering me along in each of your own special ways. I'm so lucky.

Finally, thank you over and over to Carter Seibels Singh of Bead Trust, Chris Pomeroy of Tierra Cast, Linda Hartung of Alacarte Clasps, Nina Cooper of Nina Designs, Jess Lincoln of Vintaj, Cynthia Deis of Ornamentea, Andrew Thornton of Green Girls Studio, Beadalon, and Swarovski Create Your Style for supporting *Necklaceology* by generously providing materials to create the projects in this book!

Photo by Alisha Willett Referda

ABOUT THE AUTHOR

Candie Cooper is a jewelry designer with a passion for combining unique materials and color combinations, inspired by extensive travel and her years living in China. Candie is the author of *Metalworking 101 for Beaders*, *Felted Jewelry*, and *Designer Needle Felting*, all published by Lark Books. She is the host for the Public Television series called *Hands On* and has appeared on *Beads, Baubles, and Jewels*.

As a designer in the craft and hobby industry, Candie designs for various craft companies and publications. She's currently an adjunct instructor in the art department at Manchester College and also teaches creative workshops nationally for adults. She is in her third year of teaching via the Honeywell Educational Outreach program, which provides children opportunities to explore subjects like feltmaking and jewelry making. Candie earned a Bachelor's degree in Art Education and Fine Arts from Purdue University.

For a further peek at her creative life, visit www.candiecooper.com.

index

project index

*If you already know your favorite materials or proce[ss]
use this list to find projects made using specific types [of]
beads or techniques.*

Materials

Techniques